Black Hills

(Second Edition)

by

Jay Kirschenmann

Johnsburg Public Library
3000 N. Johnsburg Road
Johnsburg, Illinois 60051
815-344-0077
www.johnsburglibrary.org

Black Hills, 2nd Edition (*Tourist Town Guides*®)
© 2011 by Jay Kirschenmann
Published by: Channel Lake, Inc., P.O. Box 1771, New York, NY 10156-1771
http://www.touristtown.com

Author: Jay Kirschenmann
Copyeditor: Kate St. Clair
Cover Design: Julianna Lee
Maps: Eureka Cartography
Page Layout Design: Mark Mullin
Publisher: Dirk Vanderwilt

Front Cover Photos:
"Mount Rushmore" © iStockphoto.com/tmarvin
"Bison Roaming on the Prairie" © iStockphoto.com/YinYang
"Cathedral Spires" © iStockphoto.com/DawnDemaske
Back Cover Photo:
"Pactola Reservoir" © Jay Kirschenmann

Published in April 2011

ISBN-13: 978-1-935455-10-3

Disclaimer: The information in this book has been checked for accuracy. However, neither the publisher nor the author may be held liable for errors or omissions. *Use this book at your own risk.* To obtain the latest information, we recommend that you contact the vendors directly. If you do find an error, let us know at corrections@channellake.com

Channel Lake, Inc. is not affiliated with the vendors mentioned in this book, and the vendors have not authorized, approved or endorsed the information contained herein. This book contains the opinions of the author, and your experience may vary.

Help Our Environment!

Even when on vacation, your responsibility to protect the environment does not end. Here are some ways you can help our planet without spoiling your fun:

★ Ask your hotel staff not to clean your towels and bed linens each day. This reduces water waste and detergent pollution.

★ Turn off the lights, heater, and/or air conditioner when you leave your hotel room.

★ Use public transportation when available. Tourist trolleys are very popular, and they are usually cheaper and easier than a car.

★ Recycle everything you can, and properly dispose of rubbish in labeled receptacles.

Tourist towns consume a lot of energy. Have fun, but don't be wasteful. Please do your part to ensure that these attractions are around for future generations to visit and enjoy.

How to Use this Book

Tourist Town Guides® makes it easy to find exactly what you are looking for! Just flip to a chapter or section that interests you. The tabs on the margins will help you find your way quickly.

Attractions are usually listed by subject groups. Attractions may have an address, Web site (🖱), and/or telephone number (☎) listed.

Must-See Attractions: Headlining must-see attractions, or those that are otherwise iconic or defining, are designated with the ★ Must See! symbol.

Coverage: This book is not all-inclusive. It is comprehensive, with many different options for entertainment, dining, and shopping, but there are many establishments not listed here.

Prices: At the end of many attraction listings is a general pricing reference, indicated by dollar signs, relative to other attractions in the region. The scale is from "$" (least expensive) to "$$$" (most expensive). Contact the attraction directly for specific pricing information.

Acknowledgements

At my side during many trips to the Black Hills is my wife Jane. She hikes through the forest, climbs into caves and co-pilots the vehicle to the far corners of the region to check out nearly every attraction. For this project she kept notes while I drove, helped research the places we overlooked and kept me from getting speeding tickets by continually pointing out the posted limit. Back home she often was by my side sorting through materials and piles of notes during the many hours and days and weeks it took to put this book together. Thanks to her encouragement and support this project was completed. And thanks to the kids for making travel fun: Sasha, Kara, Becky and Sarah.

Also, thanks to the Chambers of Commerce in each city of the Black Hills for providing the historical background for each of their towns, as well as the U.S. Forest Service for more details about this colorful region. Thanks to Sarah and Dick Carlson of Lead for pointing out special places, sometimes playing chauffeur, and for having us into their hilltop home. Thanks also to Jarett Bies and Keith Daggett for help and advice marketing the book. Amber Richey in Deadwood also was helpful in pointing out some unique places to dine throughout the Hills.

We met a lot of new friends in the Black Hills. They pass along their well wishes to you, the readers and travelers, invite you to enjoy the natural beauty and encourage you to have the respect it will take to preserve the regions for many generations of tourists who will follow. Whether caving, hiking or touring by automobile, carry out whatever you bring in so that this amazing natural resource remains in pristine condition for the next visitors, and the next generations.

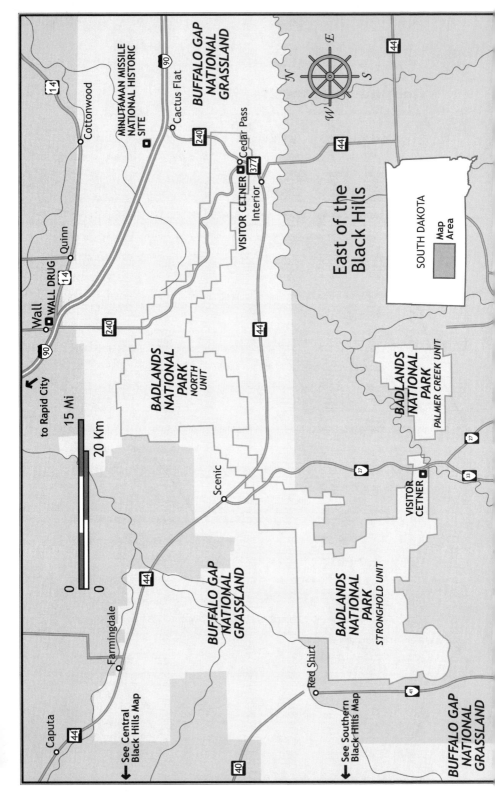

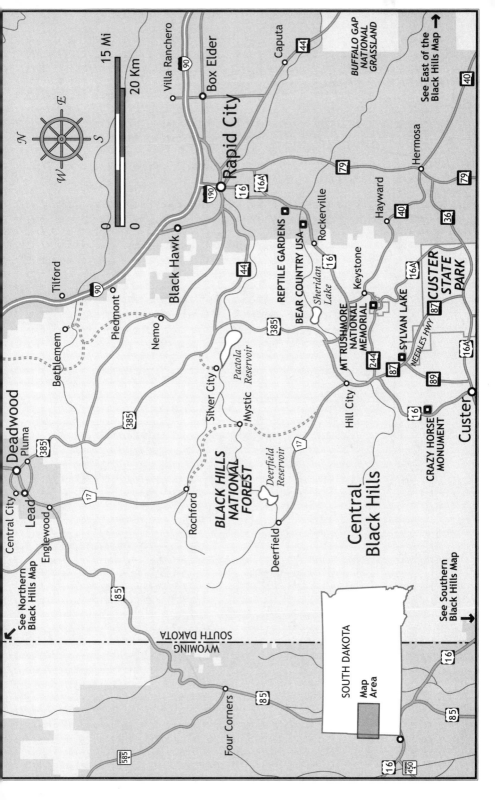

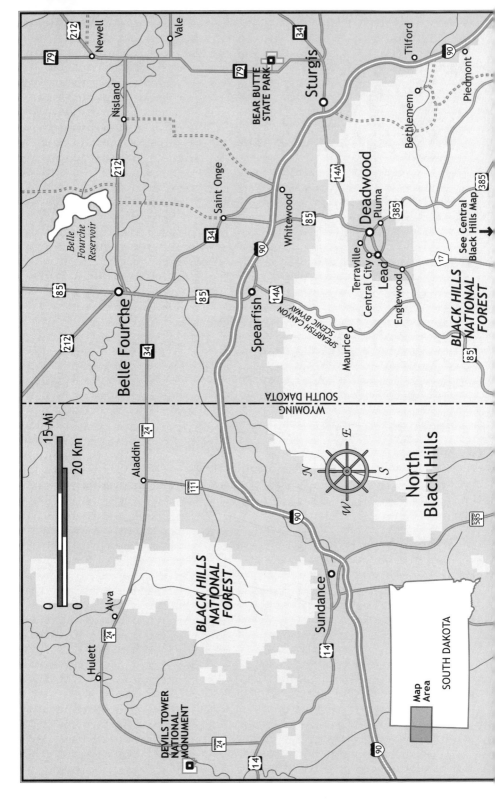

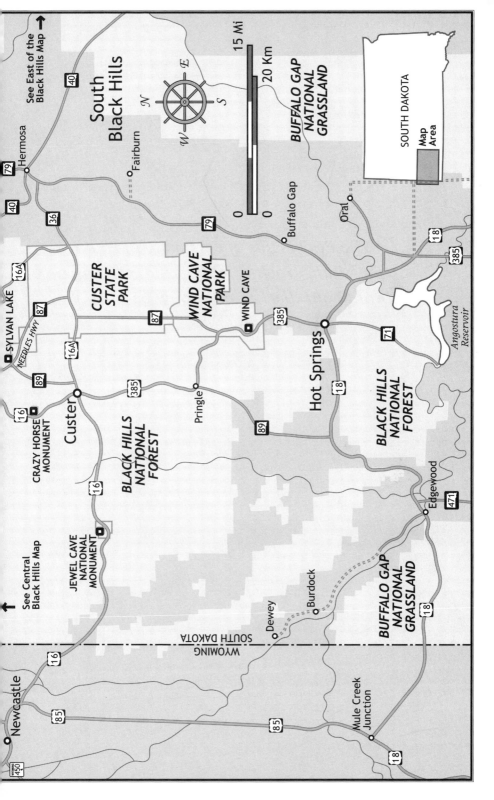

The Black Hills offers plenty of room for hiking, rock climbing and exploring throughout the 125-mile-long, 65-mile-wide region.

Table of Contents

Introduction...15

The Black Hills History.............................17

Area Orientation...23

    Getting Here 25

    Getting Around...27

    Planning Your Trip 28

    Annual Events..35

NORTHERN BLACK HILLS

Spearfish..43

    Attractions 44

    Dining...47

    Hotels 51

    Bed & Breakfasts 52

    Camping..54

    Shopping...55

Lead...57

    Attractions 57

    Ski Areas...60

    Dining...61

    Accommodations......................................64

Deadwood..67

    Bus Tours 67

    Attractions 68

    Shopping...73

    Casino Restaurants 74

    Other Restaurants...................................77

    Hotels 78

Bed & Breakfasts 81

Camping 82

Sturgis and Piedmont 85

Attractions 86

Accommodations 88

Piedmont Attractions 89

CENTRAL BLACK HILLS

Attractions in Central Black Hills 91

Hill City 101

Attractions 101

Dining 105

Hotels 107

Bed & Breakfasts 110

Camping 112

Keystone 115

Mount Rushmore and Other Attractions 115

Dining 122

Hotels 125

Bed & Breakfasts 127

Camping 129

Rapid City 131

Attractions 132

Dining 138

Accommodations 141

Shopping 142

SOUTHERN BLACK HILLS

Custer 145
    Attractions 146
    Dining..149
    Hotels 151
    Bed & Breakfasts 154
    Camping..155
Custer State Park 157
    Dining..162
    Lodging 163
Hot Springs 167
    Attractions 168
    Dining..171
    Hotels 172
    Bed & Breakfasts 175
    Camping..176

OTHER SITES AND ACTIVITIES

Outside the Black Hills 179
    Wall 182
    Northwest of the Black Hills.....................188
Outdoor Activities 193
    Hiking and Biking.......................................193
    Horseback Riding 198
    Horse Camps..201
    Golf 203
Index 207
About the Author..211

The name "Black Hills" is an English interpretation of the Lakota words paha sapa, which literally means "hills that are black."

Introduction

Welcome to the Black Hills National Forest! Nature is the star here, a place where the public is invited to explore the 1.2 million acres of heavily wooded mountains, and waving expanses of prairie grass. Buffalo (or bison), deer, elk, mountain goats, burros and other wildlife live here, sharing their home with 100 miles of national scenic byways. The Black Hills offers plenty of room for hiking, rock climbing and exploring throughout the 125-mile-long, 65-mile-wide region filled with scenic drives, lakes and waterfalls. Along the way, dozens of tourist destinations—both natural and man-made—draw thousands of visitors annually.

The Black Hills is home to the tallest peaks in continental North America east of the Rocky Mountains. Rugged rock formations, canyons and gulches situate themselves between open grassland parks, rolling streams, blue lakes and caves. The national park extends into northeastern Wyoming too, where visitors find the massive natural **Devil's Tower** stretching skyward like a 1,200-foot-tall broken Greek pillar.

The National Forest Service notes that the name Black Hills is an English interpretation of the Lakota words *paha sapa*, which literally means "hills that are black." Those thousands of acres of evergreens rising above the surrounding prairie do indeed look black, but only from far away. As you travel into the forest, colors blossom into a spectrum of greens in the pine and spruce trees, accented by white trunks of aspen and birch, and a splash of yellow, blue and purple wildflowers. Between the trees are silver, red, gray and brown rock outcroppings, with a sprinkle of the mirror-like twinkling mica rock, and white and rose-colored quartz. Throw in the dramatic visual treats of spires, cliffs and towering formations and you've got a visual feast.

The rocks in the center of the region are more than two billion years old, among the oldest in North America. Their outcroppings were sculpted by wind, water and sun to create monoliths and spires. But humans have had a hand here too. Visitors also see a spectacular view of the image known around the world: **Mount Rushmore**, the massive granite carving of four U.S. presidents' faces, located in the heart of a national forest. Standing on the observation deck and looking up at one of the world's largest works of art, visitors feel small below the four 60-foot-tall faces that keep watch over picturesque, pine-clad mountains.

It's not unusual to see deer wandering the woods and drinking from streams and lakes. Aspen leaves quiver in the wind, grass blows in waves across huge areas forever set aside as natural prairie lands where buffalo wander, prairie dogs live lives of luxury, and wild burros explore their natural surroundings. The crisp air is punctuated with the fragrance of pine, a scent that has yet to be re-created accurately. Pine is the same nostalgic aroma some may remember from fresh-cut Christmas trees hauled into the house during winter.

For hundreds of years, the Black Hills and neighboring Badlands have been sacred to Native Americans. Try to listen beyond the rumble of modern tourists' automobiles and see beyond the many attractions to appreciate the natural aura of the region. Shake off the modern world for a moment and take a different perspective. Feel the spirits of the land in this special place, a natural setting where buffalo and wild horses still roam.

The Black Hills History

The Black Hills conjures images of the American frontier, pioneers and the Old West. They embody the promise of sweeping plains, the gold rush, and the nation's westward expansion across a wild continent. Their history—or at least the iconic images of their history—has been embedded in American popular culture, in movies such as *How the West Was Won* and *Dances with Wolves*, as being in many ways the quintessential American images of exploration and conquest.

Dinosaur and woolly mammoth bones, as well as ancient evidence of past human life, are the oldest physical evidences of early activity in the Black Hills region. Archaeologists say prehistoric people were here perhaps as long as 11,000 years ago, based on the carved and painted rocks found throughout the Hills.

About 9,000 years ago, nomadic tribes of Native Americans migrated into the region along with the massive herds of buffalo (although they are technically bison, this book generally uses the local, traditional term *buffalo*) from the grasslands of the Great Plains. These roving people eventually gave way to the Arikara Indians by 1500, and later Cheyenne, Kiowa, Pawnee, Crow, and Sioux, or Lakota, according to National Park Service literature. In about 1794, the Sioux tribes achieved dominance over the Arikara.

European visitors began showing up in the region that century, starting with French explorers who claimed the land around 1700. As the United States expanded from east to west, it made the Louisiana Purchase from France in 1803, which included the

Black Hills. The next year, Lewis and Clark's expedition came through to check out the land.

European settlers, fur traders, and explorers soon followed. Much of the region where Native Americans lived was taken over. In the summer of 1867, the U.S. Congress provided a commission to work on a treaty with Native Americans, one of many attempts to buy or make deals for the land. The agreement was signed in 1868 at Fort Laramie. It gave Native Americans the Black Hills and all of what is now South Dakota, west of the Missouri River, as a reservation.

But money and greed changed everything. Around 1874, gold was discovered in the Black Hills, and by 1876 a full-fledged gold rush was under way. In spite of the treaty, the lure of gold brought thousands of prospectors to the region. Within 15 years the Hills were filled with settlements, railroads, institutions, industry and agriculture. Native Americans in the Dakotas were soon relegated to other areas set up as reservations.

The U.S. government tried to settle the land dispute, offering to buy the Black Hills from Native Americans. A group led by Chief Spotted Tail set a high price on the area, which the government refused to meet. Other bands led by Sitting Bull and other chiefs refused to consider selling at any price. The army attempted to keep miners out, but there were too many, so it gave up control as fortune seekers swarmed into the Hills.

The government eventually decided to force the Sioux onto reservations, and the area continues to be the site of a legal and political confrontation. As the 1800s drew to a close, European settlers continued to move in, so some measures of protection were set up. On February 22, 1897, President Grover Cleveland established the Black Hills Forest Reserve. In 1905 the reserve was transferred to the Forest Service, an agency of the U.S. Department of Agriculture. Two years later it was renamed the Black Hills National Forest.

COLORFUL PAST

As miners set up tent villages, built shacks, houses, and moved to the suddenly booming towns, folklore about these new residents began to grow. In July 1876, Charlie Utter's wagon train filled with ladies of the evening arrived in Deadwood. Colorful characters emerged, including Madam Dirty Em and Madam Mustachio. Brothel madam and author Dora DuFran, along with her friend, Calamity Jane, are both buried in Deadwood, DuFran with her cherished parrot, Fred.

When prostitutes arrived in town, miners lined up along the street. In some instances, unsuspecting women were lured west by offers for a chance of adventure and the promise of respectable employment, only to find themselves penniless and virtually enslaved in dance halls or brothels, according to records at the Adams Museum in Deadwood.

South Dakota became a state in 1889. A year later a tragic moment in United States-Native American history happened when hundreds of Native Americans were killed at Wounded Knee, essentially ending the Indian Wars. Development of the Black Hills continued as the first railroads from the East reached there around 1906. Protection of area lands continued in 1920, when South Dakota Governor Peter Norbeck established the Custer State Park. The park encompasses thousands of acres at the southeastern edge of the Black Hills. And while the natural setting of the region is its biggest draw, a national landmark soon appeared when painter and sculptor Gutzon Borglum began work on his Mount Rushmore sculpture in 1927. The massive piece was completed in 1941. Work on another, much larger mountain is ongoing at nearby Crazy Horse Memorial, where carving began in 1948.

GOLD MINING

Gold was discovered in the Black Hills in 1874, and the search for the precious metal defined the region for 130 years. One of America's last great gold rushes occurred in the Black Hills, at the time one of the last unexplored areas in the United States. Those early fortune seekers set up camps, shacks and the early roots of the towns that still remain today. Big business got involved too. There were several mines in the area, including the Laura Mine and the Prince Oscar Lode. In the 1870s, the Homestake Gold Mine began operations at Lead and became the largest single producer of low-grade ore for gold bullion in the world.

At the peak of gold mining years, mining magnate George Hearst owned and operated Homestake and other mines throughout the Black Hills, and more mines around the world. His techniques revolutionized mining technology. The wealthy California businessman and U.S. senator was the father of newspaperman William Randolph Hearst.

Today in Deadwood, just east of Lead, the Adams Museum has most of Homestake's records, which tell the history of the largest, oldest and deepest mine in the Western Hemisphere. The Homestake collection includes thousands of historic photographs and glass negatives, architectural drawings, maps of the mine and area, blueprints and patents, geological records of the Black Hills, original correspondence and daily journals. The mine ceased operation in 2002, but surface tours and a gift shop are on site. Today the mine is being renovated into a vast underground scientific research laboratory.

BLACK HILLS GOLD

Black Hills Gold is a distinctive design of wild grapes and leaves in rose pink, green and yellow gold, used in rings, pendants and other types of jewelry made in the region. It's the official state jewelry, but Black Hills Gold is sold throughout the world. Some credit early jewelers S.T. Butler and later his son George M. Butler as the earliest makers of Black Hills Gold. According to some legends, the pattern was inspired by a French goldsmith, Heri LeBeau, who was lost in the region in the 1800s. He found running water with grape leaves floating in it, which saved his life, so LeBeau patterned the jewelry after them.

The Landstrom company has been making Black Hills Gold for more than 120 continuous years. In 1944, Ivan Landstrom bought Black Hills Jewelry Manufacturing from earlier descendents of jewelers using the distinctive patterns. Their jewelry is called Landstrom's Original Black Hills Gold Creations. Today, several companies make Black Hills Gold in manufacturing plants and jewelry shops.

THE BLACK HILLS TODAY

The economy of the Black Hills has changed from mining and timber to today's hospitality and tourism. There is a diverse population here, a mix of both residents and visitors. The thousands of acres of natural forest and grasslands attract nature enthusiasts. Rapid City draws more urban residents, there's a military presence at the Ellsworth Air Force Base near

Rapid City, and a continual stream of tourists seek out Mount Rushmore, caves and other attractions. Ranching is still a vital part of the economy and lifestyle in this region west of the Missouri River, contributing to a cowboy-like look to rural residents, notably their clothing. You'll see a lot of cowboy hats worn by locals in small-town cafes.

The annual Sturgis Motorcycle Rally brings another element to the Black Hills for a few weeks each fall. Whether participants are "real bikers" or not, many wear the leather-and-bandanna look, and join in the multiday live music and drinking party. Some tourists choose to avoid the area during the rally season each year.

The first telephone exchanges were set up in the Black Hills in 1878, and by the early 1900s there were more than 400 phones in the state. Farmers didn't have service, however, until a rural telephone program was set up in 1949. Like anywhere else in the country, there are landlines everywhere now, but cellular telephone service still is lacking in many areas here.

Buffalo, nearly hunted to extinction, are making a comeback today. There were an estimated 60 million buffalo roaming the Great Plains for hundreds of years, but by 1889, when South Dakota became a state, they were nearly hunted to extinction. Modern buffalo ranches and wild areas like Custer State Park now serve as preserves for the massive animals, and tourists like to come out for a look. There also are buffalo on the grasslands at Wind Cave National Park, and in Badlands National Park. They're impressive to look at, but officials warn that buffalo are not domesticated like cattle—they're still wild, can be dangerous if approached by people, and can outmaneuver a horse.

Area Orientation

The Black Hills is a mountainous and heavily forested area mostly in South Dakota. The region is about 120 miles from north to south along the state's western border, with the highest and oldest rocks, peaks and gulches at its center. It's a hiker's haven, from short and easy jaunts to several-hour demanding trails in dozens of areas. The South Dakota Centennial Trail is 111 miles long, running the length of the Black Hills from Bear Butte State Park in the north to Wind Cave National Park in the south. The George S. Mickelson Trail is also more than 100 miles, from Lead-Deadwood to the southern end of the Black Hills at Edgemont.

Mount Rushmore, where four U.S. presidents' faces are carved in a granite mountain, is probably the most famous landmark in the Black Hills. And nearby, work continues with dynamite blasting on another South Dakota mega-sculpture, **Crazy Horse Memorial**, much larger than Rushmore. It's an ongoing project to honor Native Americans.

Natural beauty is the prime attraction of the Black Hills, but along the pleasant byways are many tourist destinations, too, including long-time favorites **Reptile Gardens**, **Bear Country USA**, and several Wild West towns. The area also offers a real 1880s-era train that takes sightseers on a winding ride between Hill City and Keystone along a historic stretch of track.

Gaming fans crowd into the dozens of casinos in Deadwood, which also offers restaurants, a few shops, a museum and historical sites. Actors recreate gunfights on the same streets where Old West legendary characters, including Wild Bill Hickok and

Calamity Jane, once walked (those two are buried, among other celebrities, at an often-visited final resting place, Deadwood's **Mount Moriah Cemetery**).

There's a lot to see during driving tours through the Black Hills. One mandatory drive is along **Needles Highway**, a narrow, winding road through mountainous geological formations. In some areas the road narrows to single-lane tunnels that were blasted through rock outcroppings. The road offers glimpses of Mount Rushmore, sections where the two-lane road splits into a single-vehicle path through the forest, and the historic Pigtail Bridges, where the roadway loops around and under itself.

Caves beneath the Black Hills are famous as well. **Jewel Cave** and **Wind Cave** are the second- and fourth-largest cave systems in the world. Regular guided tours show visitors the narrow passages and caverns in an underground world that twists and turns for miles. Care is taken to keep it in the same condition as it was thousands of years ago.

Travelers who take the drive eastward find the otherworldly **Badlands National Park**, just south of Wall. A roadway follows the natural contours of cliff ridges created from millions of years of wear by wind, rain and weather, which cut spires and canyons into this stark, barren land. The 244,000 acres of eroded buttes, pinnacles and spires are dotted with scenic overlooks that offer great photo opportunities, and the trailhead of paths for hikers of many skill levels.

There are lots of places for winter sports in the Black Hills too. Seasonal snow often falls several feet deep, affording plenty of opportunities for snowmobiling, snowshoe hikes and skiing, both downhill and cross-country.

GETTING HERE

If you live far from the Black Hills, flying into Rapid City is probably the fastest way to reach this central U.S. destination. There are alternatives to Rapid City's airport, but Rapid City is the largest hub. The other town airports are very small, usually used by charter and private planes.

Trains no longer bring passengers to the Hills. Take the bus as a less timely way to travel, but you'll have to rent a car or take other bus tours once you get here because of the vast distance between attractions. People who like to see the countryside along the way drive themselves, since a vehicle is needed to get around the region.

AIRPORTS

The **Rapid City Regional Airport** (☎ *605.393.2850* 🖱 *rcgov. com/airport/pages, airport code: RAP*) has direct commercial flights from several larger U.S. cities using major airlines. There are smaller airstrips used by private, corporate and general-aviation aircraft in the region. Rapid City is the recommended airport for most out-of-state tourism to the Hills.

There are other airports, however. Spearfish has the Black Hills Airport, also called **Clyde Ice Field** (☎ *605.642.4112* 🖱 *airnav. com/airport/KSPF*), while nearby is **Sturgis Municipal Airport** (☎ *605.347.3356* 🖱 *airnav.com/airport/49B*). Well east of the Black Hills is the **Wall Municipal Airport** (☎ *605.279.2666* 🖱 *airnav.com/airport/6V4*), and at the southernmost area is **Hot Springs Municipal Airport** (☎ *605.745.3135* 🖱 *airnav.com/airport/KHSR*).

AUTOMOBILE

Cruising in your auto is the best way to cover a lot of ground and still feel like you're having a close-up look at the Black Hills. The roads are fun to drive, well maintained, paved and smooth. There are back trails for those with vehicles geared for bumpy gravel and off-road experiences.

The major highway to the Black Hills from the east and west is Interstate 90, much of which was built over a wagon trail across the state. Within the Hills, drivers get around on U.S. Highways 14, 16 and 385, and South Dakota State Highways 40, 44, 71, 79, 87 and 89.

There are impressive curves, grades and areas where the road actually is blasted through rock. During the summer, driving the roadways doesn't usually pose any problems, other than the required attention to safety, and some overcrowding during peak summer weeks.

Major roads are open all winter. Some smaller roads are closed and not cleared, but still are used by snowmobiles and for other winter activities, including snowshoeing and cross-country skiing.

There are many car rental options in the Hills, especially based in Rapid City. Enterprise, Avis, Budget, Alamo and Hertz are among the services at the Rapid City airport. Many others are elsewhere in the city. Check your favorite car rental company to see if they have a location nearby.

BUS LINES

Greyhound (☎ *800.231.2222* 🖱 *greyhound.com*) crosses the country and makes its way through the region, but it won't take you to the attractions and dozens of interesting stops throughout the Black Hills. It's more a way to arrive, then rent a vehicle for your day trips. Get fare and schedule information by calling. **Jefferson Bus Lines** *(☏ 612.359.3400 🖱 jeffersonlines. com)*, based in Minneapolis, also has lines that run to Rapid City from several other major cities in the Midwest.

Also in Rapid City, which is the largest city in the region, there are in-city buses and a **trolley system** *(☏ 605.394.6631 🖱 rapidride.org)*.

GETTING AROUND

A motor vehicle is absolutely necessary to get around in the Black Hills and the nearby Badlands, whether you drive, or let bus tour companies or touring taxis services do the driving. The only public transportation is within the city limits of Rapid City, and Deadwood provides trolley service from hotels to the downtown area for a small fee. Deadwood also has several sight-seeing bus tours that leave from downtown locations. There are lots of maps available at nearly every stop throughout the Hills.

SIGHTSEEING BUS TOURS

While bringing your own car or renting one gives you the freedom to explore anywhere in the region on your own schedule, many sightseeing services are available for planned excursions into the Black Hills or Badlands. Leaving the driving to someone else makes it easier to gaze out the window at the forest and mountain vistas.

A variety of tours and planned activities, including a Mount Rushmore and Crazy Horse Memorial package, are available from **Rapid City Tours** (☎ *888.315.7913* 🖱 *rapidcitytours.com*). **Black Hills Adventure Tours** (☎ *605.209.7817* 🖱 *blackhillsadventuretours.com*) has a range of offerings, from family-friendly adventure tours to specialty tours for the more extreme outdoor enthusiasts. Some tours are narrated, like the **Golden Circle Tours** (☎ *605.673.4349* 🖱 *goldencircletours.com*).

Along with their general tours, some companies offer very specific packages for certain experiences, like the Mount Rushmore Fireworks Spectacular tour in July, and the Buffalo Round-Up Tour offered by **Gray Line of the Black Hills** *(1600 E. St. Patrick St.* ☎ *605.342.4461* 🖱 *blackhillsgrayline. com).* Concentrating on Custer State Park, Deadwood and the many scenic byways scattered throughout the region is **Mount Rushmore Tours** *(2255 Fort Hayes Dr.* ☎ *888.343.3113* 🖱 *rushmoretours.com).*

General tours of the region are offered by **Attraction Tours of the Black Hills** *(4312 Circle Dr.* ☎ *605.388.0888).* If you want food built into your trip, **Stagecoach West Tours** *(Rapid City* ☎ *605.343.3113* 🖱 *mountrushmoretours.com)* starts with a cowboy breakfast followed by a nine-hour tour of the Black Hills, Mount Rushmore, Crazy Horse Memorial and Custer State Park, with a stop at the State Game Lodge for lunch. It ends with a Western feast back at the Fort Hays Chuckwagon.

PLANNING YOUR TRIP

Most Black Hills attractions are open during the summer tourist season, from May through September. June, July and August temperatures are hot and the region is crowded. Even though it's hot during the day, bring some warm clothing, especially if you're camping, because the evenings can be cool. Some say avoiding the crowds by visiting in early spring and into the fall makes for a more relaxed experience, usually during weeks when most children are still in school.

The average Black Hills length of stay for visitors is four days and three nights in the region. If you need help brainstorming your visit, or want to make reservations, a one-stop place to book vacation packages is the site 🖱 blackhillsvacations.com, an online reservations system for the Black Hills & Badlands.

A few other groups that can help with overall plans to visit attractions are the **Rapid City Convention & Visitors Bureau** (☎ *605.343.1744* 🖱 *visitrapidcity.com*), and the **Black Hills, Badlands, and Lakes Association** (☎ *605.355.3600* 🖱 *blackhillsbadlands.com*).

SEASONS AND TEMPERATURES

The weather in the Black Hills can change quickly during all four seasons. The summer months of July and August are the warmest, with temperatures averaging about 85° Fahrenheit. Several blazing days often push into the 90s. But the humidity is low, there is usually a breeze, and most of the hot days feel cool in the shade. Nights and early mornings are cool, in the 40s or 50s, so a jacket or sweater may be needed if you're going to be outside.

Spring and fall days can warm up to 60°F or 70°F on average, but have coats and sweaters ready for chilly 45°F nights with even lower, freezing temperatures in early spring and late fall. But these seasons are a nice break from the heat of summer.

Because of its mountainous geography, winter weather has many challenges, from well-below-zero temperatures to sudden snowstorms. Visitors have to be ready to deal with changes. The winter weather can go from sunshine with mild temperatures in the mid-40s to mid-50s, to raging blizzard in just a few hours. Meteorologists say that forecasting in the Black Hills from November to March is a huge challenge.

Average winter temperatures during the coldest months of December and January are about 34°F. An average February high is just more than 38°F, with a low of 15°F. Some strange things can happen in this region, which some call "the banana belt" of the state, with peaks like the warmest recorded temperature for February of 75°F in recent decades, the National Weather Service reports.

Skiers, snowboarders, snowmobilers and snowshoe enthusiasts know how to dress in layers for the sudden changes. While there are moderate winter days, the lowest temperature in recent decades was 34°F below zero, and winter months can average 27 days with temperatures below freezing. Snowfall measurements vary greatly too. While Rapid City will get around three feet of snow during a season, the Terry Peak Ski Area can get up to three times that amount.

Check the latest weather conditions online at the **National Weather Service's Rapid City Bureau** (🖱 *crh.noaa.gov/unr*) and on a private website (🖱 *blackhillsweather.com*). For driving conditions in South Dakota, call 866.697.3511; or within the state call 511.

PACKING FOR YOUR TRIP

If you're reading this, you already have a good start on bringing essentials along to the Black Hills—your travel guide!

A cell phone and charger usually are a good idea too, but be warned: there are many areas of this region that have no service. Other areas are served by only one or two carriers, so check with yours to see if the phone will work here, or what kind of charges you may face. Folks dependent on standard cell phone use will be frustrated in many areas that have no service.

While GPS navigation equipment is great when visiting cities that tourists are unfamiliar with, the technology doesn't work well in the Hills. GPS helps get around Rapid City without a problem, but for some reason it just doesn't work well out in the Hills or even in some of the small towns, such as the very hilly Lead. Get ahold of some good maps, and find your way around the old-fashioned way, but not from Yahoo maps, Google Maps, MapQuest and other online sites that depend on the same GPS information. Some say newer or updated GPS software has begun to correct this.

There is a lot to photograph here, so be sure to bring a camera. If it's digital, remember the charging cord and lots of memory media to store those pictures. A journal or notebook and pen to make some notes and drawings might be fun to review later, or to keep track of places you visited, gas mileage, money spent and more.

An extra pair of eyeglasses can be a lifesaver, and don't forget your prescription medications. While there aren't many mosquitoes in the Black Hills, bug repellent might come in handy at times. If someone gets into poison ivy or other irritating plants, a tube of cortisone anti-itch cream is a smart addition.

If they're not already in your laptop, bring along addresses for sending postcards and e-mail. If you're driving, make sure to have your auto insurance card along.

Binoculars can be helpful to see wildlife. Bring a swimsuit if you enjoy splashing around hotel pools or the lakes. Remember the sunscreen, sunglasses and straw or wide-brimmed hats for the summer days. If you're going to be hiking, sturdy shoes or boots are a must, and have some sneakers along for less stressful walking. Even during the summer, the nights and early mornings are cool, so bring a coat or sweater.

ONLINE INFORMATION

For current, updated news about the goings on in the area, or to get more information to help plan your stay in general, here is a list of some helpful websites: **Black Hills National Forest** (🖱 *fs.usda.gov/blackhills*), **U.S. Forest Service** (🖱 *fs.fed.us/bhnf*), **Black Hills Badlands & Lake Association** (🖱 *blackhills-badlands.com*), **South Dakota Department of Tourism** (🖱 *travelsd.com*), **Black Hills Portal** (🖱 *blackhillsportal.com*), **All Black Hills** (🖱 *allblackhills.com*) and **Black Hills Tourist Information** (🖱 *blackhillstouristinfo.com*).

MAPS

Drivers, hikers, bicyclists and hunters and those in need of specific types of maps will find many specialized maps online through the **U.S. Forest Service** (🖱 *fs.fed.us/r2/blackhills/maps*).

NEWSPAPERS

The region has a newspaper in nearly every town. The major publication is the **Rapid City Journal** (🖱 *rapidcityjournal.com*), while the voice of Native Americans in the region is **The Lakota Country Times** (🖱 *lakotacountrytimes.com*).

HOSPITALS

There are several hospitals and medical centers throughout the Black Hills area, including the **Veterans Affairs Medical Center** *(500 N. Fifth St., Hot Springs* ☎ *605.745.2000)*, and the **Lookout Memorial Hospital** *(1440 N. Main St., Spearfish* ☎ *605.644.4000)*. The **Rapid City Regional Hospital** *(353 Fairmont Blvd., Rapid City* ☎ *605.719.1000)* has affiliate facilities in **Custer** *(1039 Montgomery St., Custer* ☎ *605.673.2229)*, **Lead-Deadwood** *(61 Charles St., Deadwood* ☎ *605.722.6101)*, **Spearfish** *(1440 N. Main St.* ☎ *605.644.4000)*, and **Sturgis** *(949 Harmon St., Sturgis* ☎ *605.720.2400)*.

The Sturgis Motorcycle Rally, held early August annually in Sturgis, boosts hotel rates and crowds in the Black Hills each year.

Annual Events

There are many annual events in the Black Hills, rounding out the daily offerings by tourist attractions. From buffalo roundups and car shows to the famous **Sturgis Motorcycle Rally**, visitor numbers in the Black Hills can surge during these events.

BLACK HILLS FAT TIRE MOUNTAIN BIKE FESTIVAL
(May ☎ 605.394.5225 ✆ bhfattirefestival.com) The Fat Tire Mountain Bike Festival is a four-day event that starts on the Friday before Memorial Day each year in Rapid City. It includes rides, races, raffles and demonstrations. The City of Rapid City's Parks & Recreation and the Black Hills Cycling Club sponsor the festival.

CRAZY HORSE MEMORIAL DAY WEEKEND
(May ☎ 605.673.4681 ✆ crazyhorse.org) At the Indian Museum of North America and Cultural Center, there is a Memorial Day weekend open house that features booths with guest artists. Admission to the entire memorial is free to residents of North and South Dakotas, Montana, Nebraska and Wyoming, although a donation of cash or three cans of food are requested.

WILD BILL DAYS
(June ☎ 800.999.1876 ✆ deadwood.org/deadwoodevents) Each year the Wild West town of Deadwood kicks off the summer with its annual Wild Bill Days celebration, featuring cowboy fast-draw championships, Wild West reenactors, and free concerts on Deadwood's historic Main Street.

CRAZY HORSE VOLKSMARCH

(June, Crazy Horse Memorial, 12151 Ave. of the Chiefs ☎ 605.673.4681 ◑ crazyhorse.org) Held during the first full weekend in June, this family event is the only time each year that the public can hike to the top of the colossal mountaintop carving. There is free admission to the memorial for volksmarchers. The organized hike is a 10K (6.2-mile) woodlands ramble to the world's largest mountain carving in progress. Up to 15,000 participants' turnaround point is on the outstretched arm directly in front of the carved face of Crazy Horse. Hikers get an up-close view of the mountain work that is blocking out the 22-story-high horse's head. There is no advance registration, but everyone must check in at the starting point.

CRAZY HORSE STAMPEDE / GIFT FROM MOTHER EARTH CELEBRATION

(June, Crazy Horse Memorial, 12151 Ave. of the Chiefs ☎ 605.673.4681 ◑ crazyhorse.org) In mid-June the Crazy Horse Memorial hosts several annual Great Plains Indian Rodeo Association events on the grounds of Crazy Horse. There's also an American Indian and Western Arts and Crafts show and sale, with about 30 artists participating.

BLACK HILLS OVERDRIVE ALL-CAR RALLY

(June ☎ 605.335.3700 ◑ bhoverdrive.com) Held throughout the region, the annual rally features organized events, car show competitions and cruises showcasing scenic drives in the Black Hills and Badlands. All kinds of car enthusiasts are involved, and owners of all registered makes and models may participate.

STURGIS CAVALRY DAYS CELEBRATION, ART SHOW

(June, Fort Meade, 1 mile east of Sturgis on Hwy 34

☎ 605.347.2556) Reenactments, a parade, an art show, a period fashion show and children's fishing all are part of this two-day annual event, billed as "history that you can touch." Fort Meade was a U.S. military post. Guided tours of the museum tell the story of the old fort while The Black Hills Mounted Shooters exhibit the Old West art of target shooting with a single-action revolver while riding horseback. Guests eat at the Cowboy Stew Cook-off, and retrace the steps of General Custer and his 7th Cavalry. Visitors partake in daily activities of life as it was in the 1880s, which includes history encampments and a quick-draw contest.

BLACK HILLS BLUEGRASS FESTIVAL

(June ☎ 605.384.4101, ext. 200 ⦿ blackhillsbluegrass.com) The Black Hills Bluegrass Festival started in 1980, and for many years was held at the Mystery Mountain Resort, just south of Rapid City. It now is held at the Elkview Campground, about five minutes from Sturgis at the Pleasant Valley exit No. 37 off of Interstate 90. The three-day event starts with a performer's reception on Friday night, followed by a Saturday full of workshops where novice performers can get information and lessons from the pros. The main entertainment is the Saturday night show. Free gospel music is performed on Sunday morning. There is a 4,300-square-foot building on site where food and beverages, but no alcohol, are available. On Saturday and Sunday mornings, breakfast is served in the building. The festival is organized by the Black Hills Bluegrass Association.

THE BLACK HILLS QUILTER'S GUILD SHOW

(June, Rapid City ● blackhillsquilters.org) The Guild's annual four-day show features members' displays of colorful works of art, and vendors are on hand with supplies and free demonstrations of quilting techniques. Streets and shops are filled with displays of quilts and hand-stitched items and accessories. The 2010 show set a record with 500 quilts shown.

CAR RALLY & DEMO DERBY

(June, Belle Fourche ● bellefourche.com/bfspecialevents.htm) The Center of the Nation Car Rally is an antique car rally usually held the second weekend in June. The rally started in 1987 with about a dozen cars, and now it has grown to attract nearly two hundred antique cars, trucks and hot rods from a 12-state area. It's billed as a family event, held in Hermann Park with live music, food booths, games and a swap meet.

FIREWORKS

(July) Find fireworks displays for the Fourth of July in Custer, Hot Springs, Lead, and Spearfish, and on July 3 at Mount Rushmore.

DAYS OF '76 RODEO

(July, North Main St., Deadwood ☎ 888.838.BULL ● daysof76.com) For nearly 90 years, this annual event in Deadwood has brought in cowboys and visitors alike. The rodeo is well known in the national circuit, named the Rodeo Association's "Small Outdoor Rodeo of the Year" four times, and "Midsize Rodeo of the Year" for 2004 through 2007. The Days of '76 was also named the "2007 Badlands Circuit Rodeo of the Year."

THE BLACK HILLS ROUNDUP RODEO

(July, Belle Fourche, just north of Spearfish ☻ bellefourche.com)
Held during the July 4th holiday, this is one of America's oldest rodeos. Begun in 1918, the event draws fans from all over the nation. It includes a fireworks display, a parade, carnival rides and games, street dances, classes, family reunions and, of course, the three-day rodeo. More than 4,000 covered grandstand seats offer a close-up view of rodeo events interspersed with specialty acts. Top-ranked PRCA cowboys converge from all over North America, Canada and Australia to compete for prize money.

MOUNT RUSHMORE JULY 3-4 CELEBRATION

(July ☻ nps.gov/moru) Each year, on the evening of July 3, fireworks are set off from the top of the Mount Rushmore National Memorial. Festivities continue on July 4 with music in the memorial's amphitheater at 5:30 p.m. and concluding with a program and sculpture illumination at 9 p.m. Check before you make plans to attend as the fireworks have been called off during exceptionally dry times in past years.

BLACK HILLS CORVETTE CLASSIC

(July, Spearfish ☻ blackhillscorvetteclassic.com) The Corvette Classic starts on the east side of the state, in Sioux Falls, and continues with a caravan across the state to Spearfish. The Corvette Classic also travels to several Black Hills attractions.

FESTIVAL IN THE PARK ART SHOW

(July, Spearfish ☎ 605.642.7973 ☻ spearfishartscenter.org) For more than 30 years the Festival in the Park of Spearfish has attracted hundreds to this northern Black Hills city. One of the largest outdoor summer arts festivals in the upper Midwest, the event is attended by more than 20,000 people every third weekend in July. It features more than 150 arts and crafts booths and 25 food booths. Parking near Spearfish City Park is limited, so bus shuttles are available on a regular time schedule from several downtown locations and parking areas. Camping is also available in the park campground.

GOLD DISCOVERY DAYS

(July, Custer ☎ 800.992.9818 ⦿ golddiscoverydays.com) This free annual event includes an old-time fair, craft festival, children's events, parade, car show, fun run, boat races and a hot air balloon rally.

STURGIS MOTORCYCLE RALLY

(August, Sturgis ⦿ sturgismotorcyclerally.com) The Sturgis Motorcycle Rally, held early August annually in Sturgis, boosts hotel rates and crowds in the Black Hills each year with massive parties, concerts, visits by celebrities and thousands of bikers (and those who fit in by dressing like bikers). Rally week, and the week before and after, are a great time to either join the party or avoid the Hills altogether, depending on your taste.

CENTRAL STATES FAIR AND RODEO

(August, Rapid City ☎ 605.355.3861 ⦿ centralstatesfair. com) The Central States Fair is a huge 10-day regional event featuring grandstand live bands, a cattle show and sale, a two-day horse sale, rodeo, North American Sheep Dog Trials, a buffalo sale, a Western art auction and a kids' petting zoo.

GATHERING OF THE CLANS DAKOTA CELTIC FESTIVAL

(Memorial Park, Rapid City ☗ blackhillscelticevents.org) This annual festival celebrates Celtic food and music through reen-actors, Highland athletics, history and heritage booths, a Celtic marketplace and traditional foods. The Scottish & Irish Society of the Black Hills sponsors the gathering.

MICKELSON TRAIL BICYCLE TREK

(September ☎ 605.584.3896 ☗ mickelsontrail.com) More than 500 bicyclists join in this three-day, 109-mile ride each September. Named for former South Dakota Governor George S. Mickelson, the trail is reclaimed railroad beds that wind through the heart of the Black Hills from Edgemont to Lead/Deadwood. The trail has more than 100 converted railroad bridges and four rock tunnels. Its surface is primarily crushed limestone and gravel.

DEADWOOD JAM

(September ☗ deadwood.org/deadwoodevents/deadwoodjam) This mid-September jam has brought top national musical acts to Deadwood since Jon McEuen of The Nitty Gritty Dirt Band began the event in 1990.

BUFFALO ROUNDUP

(September, Custer State Pk ☗ sdgfp.info/parks/regions/custer) On a Monday in late September or early October, visitors can watch as state employees and volunteers move the park's herd of 1,600 buffalo into corrals for sorting and branding. This event attracts more than 11,000 people each year and brings media coverage from around the world. Roundup Day is open to the public. There's also an annual arts festival, with up to

150 vendors selling their fine arts and crafts, including many South Dakota-made products.

HOLY TERROR DAYS

(September, Keystone 🖱 holyterrordays.com) Arts and crafts, an 1880 costume ball, music, and a parade are part of this city festival, named after the 1800s Holy Terror Mine. There's usually a street dance featuring a band, a public bonfire, a pig roast, auction and more during the community's celebration of its mining and logging heritage.

BLACK HILLS POWWOW & ARTS EXPO

(October ☎ 605.341.0925 🖱 blackhillspowwow.com) Held in early October in Rapid City, American Indian dancers and artists from throughout the region compete in a colorful event and show at the Rapid City Civic Center. Events include hand-game tournaments, pageants, youth day activities, a walk and run, softball, and archery tournaments.

BADGER CLARK HOMETOWN COWBOY MUSIC AND POETRY GATHERING

(Late September or early October, Hot Springs 🖱 hotsprings-sd.com) Through their stories, poems, songs and tales, performers at the Badger Clark Hometown Cowboy Music and Poetry Gathering entertain and educate visitors about the Western lifestyle, from cowboys of the past to present. Evening performances are featured, and visitors can tell their own tales at an afternoon open session. There's also a cowboy chuckwagon dinner, Western gear show and jam sessions.

Spearfish

Spearfish is a cozy little town, nestled in a valley among picturesque hilly, forested surroundings. It's the gateway to the north end of the Black Hills, built along Spearfish Creek. A "must see" drive leading to the town is through the **Spearfish Canyon Scenic Byway.**

If you've been camping or hiking and are staying in the area, this is the little town where visitors can find a movie theater, do some bowling or mini-golfing or eat at a variety of restaurants. There's a Wal-Mart here, too.

More than a century old, the town was surveyed and staked out in 1876 and officially incorporated in 1888. It is sometimes known as the "Queen City" because three prominent mountain peaks, Lookout Mountain, Spearfish Mountain and Crow Peak, form a "crown" around the city.

The town got its name from Native Americans and fur traders and trappers in the early 1800s. They considered the clear and tumbling stream through the canyon a good place to spear fish. City records show that in 1877 the first store opened, along with a United States Post Office. Black Hills State University began here in 1883, and in 1893 a railroad was built through Spearfish Canyon. The route evolved to the scenic roadway that now winds through the canyon.

There are car rentals in Spearfish, including **Enterprise Rent-A-Car** *(2825 First Ave. and 814 N. Ames St.* ☏ *605.642.3755)* and **Casey's Auto Rental Service** *(*☏ *605.722.2277).*

For general information about attractions in town, contact the **Spearfish Area Chamber of Commerce** *(106 W. Kansas St.* ☎ *605.642.2626* 🖱 *spearfishchamber.org).*

ATTRACTIONS

Spearfish Canyon, leading to this northern Black Hills city, is one of the many gems of the region, with a glimpse of a waterfall or deer darting about in the forest. In town, a national fish hatchery welcomes visitors, galleries exhibit photos and artwork, and there's even an aerial tour business.

Spearfish also has some bigger city offerings for a smaller town, like the **Lucky Strike Lanes & Mini Golf** *(1740 Ryan Rd.* ☎ *605.642.7367),* the several-screen **Northern Hills Cinema** *(1830 N. Main St.* ☎ *605.642.4212)* and movie rentals at **Mr. Movies of Spearfish** *(313 W. Jackson Boulevard* ☎ *605.722.6014).*

SPEARFISH CANYON SCENIC BYWAY ⊗ Must See!

Flanked by towering limestone cliffs and lush forest, this 20-mile route along U.S. Highway 14A is a great way to see the canyon. A forest of spruce, pine, aspen, birch and oak fills in around the roadway, and Spearfish Creek flows along the canyon bottom. It's not unusual to see deer, even during daylight hours. Bridal Veil Falls and Roughlock Falls are favorite spots to stop along the route. Allow about 40 minutes for the drive, longer with stops for hiking or photos.

The byway is naturally attractive during summer months, and shows off all the fall yellows, reds and golds as the weather begins to cool. Cheyenne Crossing Store, a stopping point on the road since the days of stagecoach traffic, still attracts travelers looking for breakfast, lunch or a rest stop.

HIGH PLAINS WESTERN HERITAGE CENTER
(I-90 Exit 14 ☎ 605.642.9378
☎ **westernheritagecenter.com)** This modern brick and glass building houses exhibits of Western art, artifacts and memorabilia. See the original Spearfish-to-Deadwood stagecoach here, along with a turn-of-the-19th-century kitchen, saddlery and blacksmith shop. There are also forestry, mining, ranching and rodeo items here, and outdoor displays include a furnished log cabin and antique farm equipment. There are more than 20,000 square feet of exhibits, including Western art.

A fully furnished, vintage rural schoolhouse in a prairie setting is on the grounds. There's also a small animal farm open during summer months, and live buffalo and longhorn cattle can be seen year-round in the pastures. Check the schedule for the Historical Campfire Series, vintage style shows, live cowboy music and poetry performances throughout the year. The building houses a 200-seat theater. ($)

D.C. BOOTH HISTORIC NATIONAL FISH HATCHERY
(423 Hatchery Circle ☎ 605.642.7730 ☎ fws.gov/dcbooth) The hatchery is located adjacent to Spearfish City Park and the city campgrounds. Set aside at least an hour to walk the grounds between displays and buildings. There is an underwater viewing area that gives visitors a face-to-face close look at trout. Established in 1896, this is one of the oldest operating hatcheries in the country that's dedicated to fish culture and resource management.

The hatchery still raises trout to stock Black Hills lakes and streams through a cooperative effort with the South Dakota state government. The hatchery also keeps fishery records and artifacts in an on-site museum. The 1907 director's house is open for tours. Grounds are open year-round from dawn to dusk, and tours of the hatchery and Booth House are open from mid-May through mid-September. It's a pleasant walk on the park-like, tree-lined grounds. The vintage Booth House is photogenic for those who like turn-of-the-19th-century architecture. Admission is free.

TERMESPHERE GALLERY

(1920 Christensen Dr. ☎ 605.642.4805 🖰 termespheres.com)
Revolving three-dimensional spheres painted by world-renowned artist Dick Termes can be seen at his gallery here in Spearfish. If he's not traveling, you probably will meet the artist. He has been creating these unique spherical paintings since 1968, works he named "Termespheres." They are exhibited in galleries around the world. See one of his works at the Deadwood History & Information Center in the old train depot in Deadwood.

It's a winding road, partially on gravel, to his three domed buildings. Call ahead for directions or if you want to make an appointment to talk with the artist. There are artistic gift items for sale, too, ranging from a few dollars to several thousand for an original Termesphere.

EAGLES' VIEW AIR TOURS

(300 Aviation Pl. ☎ 605.642.4112 🖰 eagleaviationinc.com)
Eagles' View offers 30-minute tours of Spearfish Canyon.

Longer tours fly to many other attractions in the Black Hills, and also to Devil's Tower in Wyoming. ($$$)

SPIRIT OF THE HILLS WILDLIFE SANCTUARY

(500 N. Tinton Rd. ☎ 605.642.2907 🖱 wildlifesanctuary.net)

Spirit of the Hills is a nonprofit animal rescue organization dedicated to animal welfare and advocacy. Visitors can take guided tours and nature hikes led by sanctuary volunteers. Call ahead to determine hours. ($)

DINING

Eating in Spearfish is an informal affair, with vacation attire acceptable at most establishments. You can find the usual suspects—McDonald's, Pizza Hut, Arby's, Applebee's, Perkins and the like—but look a little closer and the local flavor will emerge. There's a lot of small-town charm here, and a friendly wait staff is the norm.

SANFORD'S GRUB & PUB

(545 W. Jackson St. ☎ 605.642.3204 🖱 thegrubandpub.com)

There's a lot on the menu, with a wide selection of drinks as well. It used to be a brewpub and still is listed as such on some brewing websites, but they no longer make their own. There is a good selection of quality beers. Décor is a mishmash, with an odd but interesting assortment of random stuff on the walls. Personal favorites here include the Monte Cristo sandwich and their killer onion rings. Several visits have proven that the food here is consistently prepared as ordered and tastes wonderful. ($)

SHOOT THE BULL STEAKHOUSE

(105 S. Main St. ☎ 605.642.2848

📱 **shootthebullsteakhouse.com)** The food is delicious, the price is reasonable and the service usually is great. There's a three-sided fireplace blazing on cool days or evenings. Warm, fresh-baked bread is served before and during the meal, and on several visits so far the steaks have been cooked perfectly. The chef has been known to walk among the customers chatting and checking on food quality. ($)

BAY LEAF CAFE

(126 W. Hudson St. ☎ 605.642.5462 📱 bayleafcafe.net) Partners French Bryan and Taffy Tucker offer a nice selection of local fare and veggie options. They opened this little downtown cafe in 1993. Try an elk steak, lamb chop or one of several fish selections. There's a nice wine selection. Lots of vegetarian options are found here, including a veggie sandwich, gazpacho soup or tabbouleh salad. Excellent desserts made on site. Artwork by local artists is on the walls, changes often and is offered for sale. The building was built in 1892 as the Queen City Hotel and went through many years of neglect until rescued and remodeled by French and Taffy. ($)

SPEARFISH CANYON LODGE

(10619 Roughlock Falls Rd. ☎ 605.975.6343 📱 spfcanyon.com) Travel south on Highway 14-A a few miles from Spearfish to find this gem of a location. Don't believe your GPS system, which in some cases will try to get you to travel on Forest Service Road 222: it's a dirt road, not the famous Spearfish Canyon Byway also called 14-A. Some of the most popular waterfalls in the canyon are nearby: Roughlock Falls, Little

Spearfish Falls, and a little farther northeast is picturesque Bridal Veil Falls.

The eatery, Latchstring Restaurant, is in a separate adjacent building, continuing the rustic stone and lumber theme of the lodge. Open year-round for breakfast, lunch and dinner, it is known for its local-source food including the buffalo rib-eye, baked or pan-seared walleye and blackened trout. Many hiking trails start at the lodge, and the restaurant will prepare backpack picnics. ($$)

SPEARFISH CHOPHOUSE AND WHISKEY BAR

(523 Spearfish Canyon Rd. ☎ 605.642.1134) At the west entrance to the scenic road through the canyon, about a half mile from town, is this modest but comfortable bar that serves food. It's a natural-wood-sided, cabin-like building. Toss peanut shells on the wood floor at this sparely decorated establishment where the food is consistently good. Try the tenderloin medallions with the garlic mashed potatoes. ($/$$)

ROMA'S RISTORANTE

(2281 E. Colorado Blvd. ☎ 605.722.0715 ⬦ romasristorante.net) This little restaurant was located downtown for several years, but now is near Kmart, just off Interstate 90 on Exit 14. Food here usually is consistently good, although the calamari was overdone on a recent visit. Other dishes are great. Try a local favorite, the pheasant ravioli with roasted garlic and sun-dried tomato creme sauce. Good stuff. You can't go wrong with the calzones, pizza and lasagna. Friendly staff. ($$)

LUCKY'S 13 PUB

(305 N. 27th St. ☎ 605.642.4683) Locals agree that, for a little hotel restaurant (Lucky's 13 is within the **Spearfish Holiday Inn Convention Center)**, this casual-dining spot has great food. There is a terrific selection of beer on tap. Rough brick walls and dark wooden furniture in Lucky's 13 Pub make for a cozy atmosphere. It serves meals typical of bar food, but with good-sized portions. ($/$$)

CEDAR HOUSE RESTAURANT

(130 Ryan Rd. ☎ 605.642.2104) Cedar House features good Mom & Pop-style dining—good food at good prices, in a quiet restaurant. Sirloin steak tips here are a favorite. Homemade soups are delicious. ($)

GUADALAJARA MEXICAN RESTAURANT

(83 W. Hwy 14 ☎ 605.642.4765) The owners are a couple from Guadalajara, Mexico. He was a former professional in the national soccer league there, so there are many photos of teams on the walls. Food is excellent and service is good, with your waitperson stopping by the table often to see how things are going. The staff lightens the atmosphere with some good-natured joking around with customers. ($)

GREEN BEAN COFFEEHOUSE

(304 N. Main St. ☎ 605.717.3636) This is a converted house with comfortable outdoor porch seating. Inside, an eclectic collection of old tables and chairs make for a cozy place to try one of many coffee drinks. Choose from a wide selection of fresh sandwiches, including wraps, panini and grilled offerings. It's a fun place to take a break, get some fresh-brewed coffee and hang around with a mix of laptop-absorbed college students and an assortment of regular, local customers. ($)

HOTELS

One of the nicest lodges in the region is in the canyon—Spearfish Canyon Lodge. Visiting the lodge puts you into nature, continuing the earthy feel from outside to the inside, with rock and wood furnishings. Travelers on a budget can find comfortable accommodations at motels in town too.

BEST WESTERN BLACK HILLS LODGE

(540 E. Jackson Blvd. ☎ 605.642.7795) Visitors find clean rooms at this roadside motel. It's an affordable place for families on a budget, and there are a few perks like free wireless Internet and satellite TV with lots of channels. Bathrooms have an outside vanity area with plenty of counter space, and some rooms feature a large hot tub. There's also an indoor whirlpool and sauna. The swimming pool is outdoors. Free continental breakfast is served, including fruit, toast, cereals, juice, milk, coffee and a waffle bar. ($)

TRAVELODGE OF SPEARFISH

(346 West Kansas St. ☎ 605.559.3333
☋ travelodgeofspearfish.com) Located in downtown Spearfish, in a quiet residential neighborhood with adjacent parks, this Travelodge offers large clean rooms that include a safe. The shower has bowed curtain rods so there is more elbow room. Standard continental breakfast with the make-your-own waffle feature is available. Recent remodeling makes for a nice feel. There's a tiny casino, and a living room area with a fireplace.

Pets are permitted in certain rooms for a small extra charge. Friendly staff. ($)

SPEARFISH CANYON LODGE ✪ Must See!

(10619 Roughlock Falls Rd. ☎ 605.975.6343 🐭 spfcanyon.com)
Even if you don't stay here, stop in and check it out. This lodge is close to area waterfalls. Take time to walk through the main hall of this lodge constructed from rock and wood. Soaring beamed ceilings, heavy log walls and a huge, rustic stone and lumber fireplace make for an amazing room just off the front desk. Visitors who decide to stay have a choice of 54 luxury rooms and suites, open all seasons. All rooms have either king or queen pillow-top beds with warm comforters. The lodge provides lots of scenery viewable from oversized windows. There are several enjoyable hikes on short, easy trails that lead from the lodge to various waterfalls in the canyon. ($$)

BED & BREAKFASTS

For some folks, the homey feel and personal service of a bed and breakfast is a favorite way to stay in the Black Hills. There are several in Spearfish and in the surrounding forests. Each offers a different experience and a different type of lodging. Many guests return year after year, saying they feel as if they are at their home away from home during visits.

YESTERDAY'S INN BED AND BREAKFAST
(735 N. 8th St. ☎ 605.644.0210 🐭 yesterdaysinn.net) This Victorian-style home is in historic downtown Spearfish. Outdoor areas feature a landscaped yard, gardens, gazebo

and a fishpond. Inside there are four rooms, two suites and a cottage. Open year-round, it's a short walk to Spearfish shops and restaurants. ($)

SECRET GARDEN BED & BREAKFAST

(938 N. Ames ☎ 605.642.4859) This brick Victorian house, built in 1892, has five rooms, each with a private bath. It's a comfortable and inviting place run by a friendly mother-daughter team who make outstanding breakfasts. Common area features a fireplace, television and game table. A laundry is available. Rates include a gourmet breakfast served in the formal dining room, the garden or in your room by request. Afternoon tea and refreshments are included. Gardens have a hot tub and gazebo with fireplace. Guests are allowed to pick vegetables from the summer garden. ($$)

SAND CREEK BED & BREAKFAST

(10366 West U.S. Hwy 14 ☎ 605.642.7251
⬤ sandcreekbedandbreakfast.com) Located on 40 acres west of Spearfish, this house has four bedrooms, each with its own bathroom. The master bedroom has a whirlpool tub. A summerhouse is located away from the main house—very small, with no inside plumbing or running water. A home-cooked breakfast is served in the family kitchen each morning, included in the standard rates. The owners say they can meet special dietary needs upon request. Guests can hang around in the hammock on the large wraparound porch, and those who bring along horses can use the barn with two box stalls for an additional fee. Runs are available, or ride in most of the 40-acre grounds, in a large outdoor riding arena, or on nearby U.S. Forest Service land. There's a two-night minimum stay. ($/$$)

CAMPING

Living life a little closer to nature is easy in this region, but many sites also have modern perks like free wireless Internet access for those who want to stay connected to the world. Tents, cabins and RV campers have plenty of choices in the Spearfish area, from multi-lot parks and cabins to scattered tent sites for those who don't like to be too close to each other.

ELKHORN RIDGE RV RESORT & CABINS

(20189 US Hwy 85 ☎ 605.722.1800 📱 elkhornridgervpark.com)
Elkhorn Ridge is a full-service, 75-acre RV resort with 186 paved sites, 36 fully furnished cabins (24 with kitchenettes) and 20 tent sites. It's a modern resort with free Internet, cable television, fire pits and a fenced-in dog area with separate sections for small and large dogs. The lodge building has a gift shop and general store. There's an outdoor heated pool, kiddie pool, two hot tubs, lighted tennis, volleyball and basketball courts, and horseshoe pits.

MOUNTAIN VIEW CAMPGROUND

(625 Christensen Dr., exit 14 off I-90 near Spearfish ☎ 605.642.2170 📱 mountainview-campground.com) Mountain View has a convenience store, a big heated pool, wireless Internet access, showers and lots of shade from mature trees. One-room cabins are available that include a microwave, small refrigerator and window air conditioning.

SPEARFISH CITY CAMPGROUND

(625 Fifth St. ☎ 605.642.1340 📱 spearfishparksandrec.com)
This nicely shaded campground is nestled along Spearfish

Creek, an excellent trout fishing stream. It is located adjacent to the D.C. Booth Historic Fish Hatchery and Spearfish City Park. Within walking distance of the campground is downtown Spearfish, with public laundry facilities, grocery stores, hardware stores and the Matthews Opera House. The site has soda and ice machines, Internet access, picnic tables, grills and a sewer dump station. There are more than 60 RV hookup sites, and 150 non-hookup sites.

SHOPPING

Spearfish is a small town but with a little wandering, visitors can find some interesting shops. There are clothing stores, furnishing and home decor stores, general retail sales, liquor stores, department stores, tool and hardware shops, and a few gift and novelty shops. The town has a relaxing, slow pace. For those who can't live without the big-box chain, there's a **Wal-Mart** *(285 First Ave.)* in town.

FOCUS WEST GALLERY
(939 Colorado Blvd. ☎ 605.722.0708 🖱 focuswestgallery.com)
Award-winning nature photographer Les Voorhis owns the Focus West Gallery with his wife. Browse his images of the Black Hills and other photographic artwork from 9 a.m. to 6 p.m., closed from 1 to 2 p.m., Tuesday through Saturday.

DAKOTA QUILT COMPANY
(1004 N. Main St. ☎ 605.642.2939 🖱 dakotaquiltcompany.com)
Quilters who are on the road and short on supplies will find fabrics, books, patterns and notions here. Folks staying longer can check out the classes. Sewing machines are sold here, too,

along with embroidery supplies. Waiting families are invited to explore the landscaped grounds around the shop, including patchwork flowerbeds and peaceful nooks.

Lead

Pronounced "leed," this is a hilly place, high in the Black Hills, with many of its houses and buildings perched precariously on steep inclines. It's the quiet neighbor, just down the road from partying sister-city Deadwood. The town was officially founded in July 1876, after the discovery of gold brought miners to the area. The name *Lead* comes from a mining term that refers to an outcropping of gold-bearing ore, or as some like to say, "Lead the miners to the mother lode."

Lead is a slow-moving residential town, a tough place to ride bicycles because of the hills. This is where the **Homestake Gold Mine** rose to fame, closed, and now is being converted to a scientific research center. Learn about Lead's rich gold-mining history in places like the **Black Hills Mining Museum**, which provides an inside look at mining and its history. Along Main Street, stores offer jewelry, collectibles and antiques, restaurants and pubs, art galleries and the **Historic Homestake Opera House**. Historic homes and buildings line Main Street.

For general information about Lead, contact the **Lead Area Chamber of Commerce** *(160 W. Main St. ☎ 605.584.1100 ♟ leadmethere.org).*

ATTRACTIONS

There are both summer and winter offerings here, with a premier ski resort nearby for cold-weather visitors. Tour what was once one of the largest gold mines in the United States.

HOMESTAKE MINE

(160 W. Main St. ☎ 605.584.3110

🖱 **homestaketour.com, homestakevisitorcenter.com)** Visitors are not taken underground during this tour of the famous Homestake Mine that closed in 2002. For now the best look at the area is an hour-long bus tour available on the grounds. Stops include a walk-through of some of the buildings and a look at remaining equipment. See where the mining process occurred, included hoisting, crushing and milling of the gold ore brought up from underground. The tour bus also travels through the historic town of Lead, with a guide pointing out areas of interest.

Homestake is the deepest mine in the United States, reaching a depth of more than 8,000 feet. Today the mine is being renovated into an underground scientific research laboratory. With more than 375 miles of tunnels, scientists say it will make a perfect research lab. So far, millions of dollars in funding has been secured for the Sanford Underground Science and Engineering Laboratory at Homestake. Key to the location are the deep tunnels, where thousands of feet of rock shields the experiments from cosmic rays and other background radiation. While there are no public tours of the lab yet, those interested may read lots of details about the scientific project online (🖱 *sanfordundergroundlaboratoryathomestake.org)*. ($)

BLACK HILLS MINING MUSEUM

(323 W. Main St. ☎ 605.584.1605 🖱 mining-museum.blackhills. com) The Mining Museum is a nonprofit educational attraction that shows many of the tools and equipment used for mining. There are historic photographs and mining artifacts from the region's more than 130-year mining history. The collection dates from when people first tried to make a fortune on their own when more modern equipment was used by companies setting up large operations. Former Homestake gold miners built a timbered passage that simulates an underground gold mine. The museum is open daily with a limited winter schedule. Visitors can try gold panning, and the museum guarantees that they will find a little gold. A gift shop includes apparel, books and panning supplies. ($)

PRESIDENT'S PARK

(Deer Mountain Rd. off Hwy 85 🖱 presidentspark.com) At President's Park, located about four miles south of Lead, visitors find 42 giant busts of U.S. presidents arranged in chronological order. Watch for the giant Lincoln sculpture at the entrance. The sculptures, 20 feet tall, are arranged along a landscaped park setting. It takes about an hour to walk through the entire park, more if you plan to eat there or peruse the visitors center. Artist and sculptor David Adickes, who was inspired by Mount Rushmore to create sculptures of all the presidents, made the artwork. Each bust has a biographical panel and state flag. There's also a garden café, and picnic tables for those who bring their own food. The visitors center and gift shop carries lots of American-themed items and books. Open year-round. ($)

HISTORIC HOMESTAKE OPERA HOUSE

(309 Main St. ☎ 605.584.2067 🖱 leadoperahouse.org) Known as the "Jewel of the Black Hills," the Opera House has been a landmark in this small mining town for nearly a century. It was built in 1914, providing a venue for live theater, and housing a recreation center for yesterday's miners and their families. The opera house has endured two major fires, and today the structure is undergoing massive reconstruction to restore the interior theater and recreation building. Concerts and community theater shows are often presented here. Call or check online for current schedules and tours.

SKI AREAS

For the vertically inclined, the Lead area is a good place to experience some of the Black Hills' area ski resorts.

TERRY PEAK SKI AREA

(21120 Stewart Slope Rd. ☎ 605.722.7669 🖱 terrypeak.com)
Open in late November as snowfall permits, the Terry Peak Ski Area was founded in 1938. More consistent skiing started when the attraction started making snow in the 1970s to cover the slopes during the Black Hill's unpredictable winters. This is one of the highest areas in the region. The summit of Terry Peak stands at 7,076 feet, with the highest vertical drop between the Rockies and the Alps. There are accommodations across the road at **Barefoot Resort**. During the mid-2000s, the ski area saw the largest terrain expansion in more than 25 years, adding about 100 acres of new trails. There are runs for beginner, intermediate, and expert skiers and snowboarders.

Once the snow melts, Terry Peak opens up trails several weekends for downhill mountain biking. Ride the lift up, check out the spectacular mountaintop view, then take the designated trails downhill. Summer hiking also is available, Monday through Thursday. ($$)

MYSTIC MINER SKI RESORT / DEER MOUNTAIN

(11187 Deer Mountain Rd. ☎ 605.584.3230 🖱 skimystic.com)
Mystic Miner Ski Resort at Deer Mountain offers winter
tubing, snowboarding, skiing and sleigh rides. On the grounds
for year-round use is the Mine Shaft Tavern, a full-service
coffee bar and restaurant. The summit is 6,850 feet high,
and day hikers can explore the 44 trails there. Check out the
learning center, and the Atomic Shelf Terrain Park with a
variety of features. Blizzard Park here is one of the largest
winter tubing park in the Hills, with multiple tubing lanes.
Children younger than age 5 get in free with paying adults but
must be at least 42 inches tall to slide on the hills. Tubes and
rides to the top of the attraction are provided. ($$)

DINING

Grab a cheeseburger and beer at **Lewie's**, or plan a classy sit-
down feast at the **Roundhouse**, one of the newest restaurants
in the Black Hills. There's a popular little coffee shop here, too,
among other offerings.

LEWIE'S SALOON & EATERY

(711 S Main St. ☎ 605.584.1324) The address says "Main
Street," but this little restaurant-pub is actually a short drive
southwest, outside of the city proper on U.S. Highway 14/85
and nestled on a tree-filled hill. This is a casual place to grab
an excellent hamburger in a cozy atmosphere in the front, with
a large bar at the back. Recommended by locals. Take time to
look around on the walls, all the way up the vaulted ceiling:
They're covered with an eclectic collection of items including

huge gas-powered saws once used to cut lumber in the area, '60s era games and some photos. ($)

STAMPMILL INN AND RESTAURANT

(305 W. Main St. ☎ 605.584.1984 🖱 tvoco.com/stampmill)
Stampmill is a comfortable, century-old building, serving a limited menu of American-style seafood and steak. The restaurant features an extensive Sunday brunch that includes watching the chef make custom omelets. Cajun fans will like the excellent jambalaya pasta. It's a plain-looking building along the historic Main Street. If the weather is nice, sit outside on the patio next to the building to watch a little Main Street traffic. The four-story brick structure was built as a boarding house in 1897 and has since undergone renovation. Above the restaurant are two-room suites with Victorian decor and access to an indoor hot tub. ($)

BLACK HILLS FT. PIERRE RAILROAD ROUNDHOUSE RESTAURANT ✪ Must See!

(106 Glendale Dr. ☎ 605.722.1901

🖱 blackhillsftpierrerailroadroundhouse.com) Located on Highway 14A at the top of Lead's Main Street, this 1901 railroad round-house building was recently renovated into a restaurant that seats about 135 people under grand chandeliers. Flat screens at some booth-like tables show an outdoor scene slowly passing by, as if you were riding in a train car. Favorite foods here include the spice-rubbed salmon, or the pork tenderloin with apple cranberry chantey.

There's a life-size replica of a train engine, tender box and dining car built to look like it's coming out of a mountain tunnel. The dining car is available for a sit-down meal. Service staff dresses up, females with frocks and feathered hats, males with vest and coats. Located next door to the Golden Hills Resorts and Convention Centers, the restaurant is closed on Sundays. Be sure to check out the Living Map Theater room. It's a multimedia presentation describing the Black Hills gold rush. A movie featuring historical photos and old film clips, along with live reenactments, tell the history of the area. A 24-by 28-foot 3D map on the floor lights up during the presentation, showing where the events on screen happened. It's about a half-hour show, shown on the hour throughout the day. ($$)

CHEYENNE CROSSING STORE AND B&B

(21415 US Hwy 14A, Spearfish Canyon, Lead ☎ 605.584.3510 ● cheyennecrossing.org) At the junction of U.S. Highways 14A and 385, Cheyenne Crossing feels like a small-town café. There's plenty of seating inside, but there's also outdoor seating under umbrella-equipped tables. The historic stagecoach stop offers a comfortable setting, surrounded by rock cliffs and Spearfish Creek nearby. The cook says that all food served is made from scratch. Recommended by locals, Cheyenne Crossing was twice featured in *Midwest Living* magazine's "Best Breakfast Spots in the Midwest."

Homemade sausage gravy and buttermilk biscuits, sourdough pancakes and buffalo burgers are favorites here. The Indian tacos are made with soft, warm flatbread filled with taco meat and beans, chopped tomatoes, green chilies, chopped red onion, picante sauce and a heap of sour cream on top. ($)

GRADINARU'S HAUS OF KAFFEE

(32 Baltimore St. ☎ 605.722.4670) This is a cute little shop, good for a quick stop on the way to the Terry Peak Ski Area.

Locals on their way to work often grab a cup here on the go, or settle in for a quiet moment. Gradinaru's also has chai tea. ($)

ACCOMMODATIONS

There are a few places to stay in Lead, and even more in the region around the town, providing accommodations with a country feel.

GOLDEN HILLS RESORTS & CONVENTION CENTERS

(900 Miners Ave. ☎ 605.584.1800) Rooms are clean, you can get a good steak in the restaurant, and a large buffet breakfast is available. The decor isn't fancy, but it's functional. The bar gathers a fun crowd, and there's a computer for use near the lobby where comfy leather sofas are clustered to lounge around in. If you don't want to drive, there's a mini-bus shuttle into Deadwood. Walk through an underground tunnel to the **Northern Hills Family Recreation Center** building next door, where hotel guest get free use of the pool, running track, hot tub, weight rooms, cardio area and racquetball courts. Not open Sundays. ($)

CHEYENNE CROSSING STORE AND B&B

(21415 US Hwy 14A, Spearfish Canyon ☎ 605.584.3510 ☋ cheyennecrossing.org) This location along the scenic highway covers a lot of ground. Cheyenne Crossing is a restaurant, a bed & breakfast, a gift shop and a grocery store. A little rustic at first glance, they have a good selection of breakfast items and provide a regular stop for locals as well as travelers. It's located at the junction of U.S. Highways 14A and 385.

The rooms upstairs, surrounding a central lodge, have natural wood walls and king-size beds. Twin beds and additional rollout beds can accommodate larger groups of six to eight people. They have some home-style features, such as refrigerator, satellite television, stereo, microwave and toaster oven. There's also a two-bedroom creekside cabin. Cheyenne Crossing has been a landmark since 1878, when the Deadwood-Cheyenne Stagecoach stopped here on its regular route to and from Cheyenne, Wyoming. The original building was destroyed by fire in 1960 and was replaced by this larger, more modern structure. ($)

BAREFOOT RESORT

(21111 Barefoot Loop ☎ 800.424.0225 🖱 barefootresort.com) The view from up here is spectacular, looking back across the canyon with its very rocky, tree-filled terrain. Many condos at Barefoot Resort are owned in a timeshare system, but there also are rentals by the day (two-day minimum) or week in this resort, located across from **Terry Peak Ski Area**. Room choices range from one, two and three-bedroom units, fully furnished from small appliances to television with satellite system, gas fireplaces, dishes, glassware and cooking utensils. There are two pools, two hot tubs, two exercise rooms, saunas, and a sports court that can be used for basketball, volleyball and tennis. ($$$)

RECREATIONAL SPRINGS RESORT

(11201 Hwy 14A ☎ 605.584,1228 🖱 recsprings.com) This resort, a few miles south of Lead, is nestled in the forest. There are rooms in the lodge, cabins, RV hookups and campsites. New-looking small cabins are built in a rustic way, with wood-plank interiors. There's a restaurant in the lodge, and a tattoo and piercing parlor on the premises. This is a good home base for visitors who like to hike, bicycle, snowshoe and snowmobile, go trout fishing, hunting and more. ($)

Deadwood

The Wild West town of Deadwood was founded following the discovery of gold in 1876. It was a party town back then, and continues that legacy today. There are dozens of casinos, many located in historic buildings, lining old Main Street. As a result, there's not a lot for kids to do in Deadwood.

But it's not all just casinos. Look more closely and you'll find a variety of shops, including jewelry and souvenirs. Gambling establishments also offer buffets, restaurants and gift shops.

The entire city of Deadwood is a National Historic Landmark. Re-created turn-of-the-century street lamps line historic Main Street, and many buildings are accurately restored. The cemetery here is the final resting place for Wild Bill Hickok and Calamity Jane.

Reached by railroad in 1891, the city developed as a trading center for the northern Black Hills region. The town was named for the dead trees that were found in the narrow Deadwood Gulch Canyon where Main and Sherman Streets are today.

For general information about Deadwood, contact the **Deadwood Chamber of Commerce and Visitors Bureau** *(767 Main St. ☎ 605.578.1876 🖱 deadwood.org).*

BUS TOURS

While walking along Deadwood's historic Main Street, visitors will find companies selling bus tours of the Deadwood area. Guides tell about the town's history, historic buildings and past residents.

KEVIN COSTNER'S ORIGINAL DEADWOOD TOURS

(☎ 605.578.2091 ☗ originaldeadwoodtour.com) Tickets are sold and boarding is at 677 Main Street, in front of the actor's **Midnight Star Casino** and restaurants. This tour runs every day from May to mid-October. ($)

ALKALI IKE TOURS

(☎ 605.578.3147) Alkali Ike tours are about one-hour narrated tours of Deadwood and famous Boot Hill Cemetery. Tickets are sold and boarding is in front of historic **Saloon No. 10** at 600 Main Street. ($)

BOOT HILL TOURS

(☎ 605.578.3758 ☗ boothilltours.com) Tickets are sold and boarding is at the Bodega, 662 Main St. The bus takes visitors to historic **Mount Moriah Cemetery**, also known as Boot Hill, and several other city landmarks during a one-hour narrated tour. It's an open-air bus, so pick a dry day for this tour. ($)

ATTRACTIONS

Deadwood is steeped in history, so many of the non-casino attractions are historic sites. Photos, artifacts and writings from 100 years ago are still here, displayed in area museums. A sense of who lived in Deadwood can be seen in the headstones at the local cemetery, including Wild Bill Hickok and Calamity Jane. From a tribute to buffalo at a nearby Kevin Costner attraction to a rodeo museum, there are several alternatives to casinos in and around this famous Western town.

BROKEN BOOT GOLD MINE

(Just off upper Main St. ☎ 605.578.1876

🖱 brokenbootgoldmine.com) Tours leave every 30 minutes at this 1878 mine. The guides are well versed in the early days of mining operations. Broken Boot is an authentic gold mine from the rustic days when men looked for gold by blasting black powder and searching the results by candlelight. Visitors take a tour of the mine, and afterward can pan for gold (with guaranteed results). Every guest goes home with a souvenir "share" of stock. The tour follows the former path of ore cars deep underground into the century-old mine shafts. It's rustic and dark but hey, it's a mine! This is where thousands of faceless miners sought their fortunes in the dark and explosive atmosphere of black powder and candlelight. ($)

ADAMS MUSEUM

(54 Sherman St. ☎ 605.578.1714

🖱 adamsmuseumandhouse.org) Learn how settlers lived during the early days of this Wild West town through artifacts and displays in this three-level museum. If you like history, give yourself a few hours to explore the museum's displays and exhibits, which are packed with items and pictures from the past. There are books, furniture, clothing, guns, hardware and personal objects from townspeople.

Open year-round, the eclectic collection of artwork and artifacts reflects the natural history and pioneer past of the northern Black Hills. The Adams Bros. Bookstore is on the first floor. Admission is free, although a donation is appreciated. The museum is affiliated with the nearby Adams House.

Deadwood

HISTORIC ADAMS HOUSE

(22 Van Buren Ave. ☎ 605.578.3724 ☷ adamsmuseumandhouse. org) When pioneer business leader, museum founder and builder W.E. Adams died in 1934, his wife closed the house and move to California. For a half century time stood still, with linens folded in drawers, china stacked in the cupboards and even cookies in a clear glass jar.

Late 1800s press described the home as "the grandest house west of the Mississippi." The elegant Queen Anne-style house heralded a wealthy and socially prominent new age for Deadwood, a former rough and tumble gold mining town. The guides do a good job of helping visitors understand what life was like when the family lived there. Guides point out the original features and furnishings, and what changed with the restoration project that cost $1.5 million, before it opened to the public in 2000. ($)

MOUNT MORIAH CEMETERY

(☎ 605.578.2600 ☷ deadwood.org) Now owned by the City of Deadwood, Mount Moriah Cemetery is atop a steep hill, so people who choose to walk there get a good workout. It's a tight uphill drive through narrow neighborhood streets to get to the cemetery, known for 100 years as Boot Hill, so take care rounding corners. The historic grounds, nestled amid evergreen trees, is the final resting place of folks like James Butler "Wild Bill" Hickok, Calamity Jane, Potato Creek Johnny, Preacher Henry Weston Smith, Seth Bullock, journalist Edward L. Senn, Dr. Flora Stanford, Harris Franklin (of local Franklin Hotel fame) and more. Sections are well documented, and there's a walking tour.

The city collects $1 per visitor to maintain the grounds. A walking guide comes with the admission price. It includes background on the most famous people buried there, and a large fold-out map of the grounds. There's an interesting view from the top of the hill looking down on Deadwood, so have your camera ready. ($)

TRIAL OF JACK MCCALL

(Masonic Temple, Historic Main St. ☎ 605.578.1876) If you hear gunfire, it's probably the Old West actors who hawk the 8 p.m. nightly "Trial of Jack McCall" with loud, rough shouting in the streets. The trial is preceded by a mock shootout on Main Street, from Memorial Day to Labor Day weekend. ($)

DAYS OF '76 MUSEUM

(17 Crescent St., adjacent to the Rodeo Grounds ☎ 605.578.2872 🖱 daysof76museum.com) The Days of '76 Museum began by collecting horse-drawn vehicles used in the early days of the annual **Days of '76 Rodeo Parade**, including the original Deadwood stagecoach. History and rodeo buffs find artifacts, photographs and memorabilia from more than eight decades of rodeos, as well as Native American items. It's still a pole barn, but a huge fund-raising campaign is under way to build a modern, climate-controlled museum.

TATANKA: STORY OF THE BISON

(1 mile north of Deadwood on Hwy 85 ☎ 605.584.5678 🖱 storyofthebison.com) When actor Kevin Costner finished filming *Dances with Wolves* in the region, he bought some land and built Tatanka, the attraction he wants to be the centerpiece for the Native American and European cultures. There's really not a lot to see here, but history buffs and folks interested in native and natural history will enjoy spending about an hour here. There's a short film and a talk, too. A larger-than-life bronze sculpture featuring bison (or buffalo) pursued by Native American horseback riders is built on this hill that has a great view of the northern Black Hills. The sculptures were commissioned during Costner's plans to build a mega-resort/casino called The Dunbar on the site, named after the character he portrayed in *Dances with Wolves*. The project fell through, but Costner decided to place the sculptures there anyway, and opened the educational attraction. Native interpreters and several exhibits demonstrate how the native culture depended on buffalo and how their near extinction affected the Native American culture. There's a hands-on educational center and Native American gift shop, and an indoor-outdoor restaurant. Open May through September. ($)

TROUT HAVEN

(22485 Hwy 385 ☎ 605.341.4440 🖱 trouthavenresort.com)
Situated on U.S. Highway 385 between Pactola Lake and Deadwood, the staff has raised fish here since 1952 in two man-made, fully stocked trout ponds. Travelers who like to fish don't have to bring equipment—it's all provided on site. No license is needed, and there's no limit. Cleaning is free, and the staff will pack fillets on ice or cook them on the spot. There's also a restaurant, and fishing lessons are offered by appointment. Campsites, RV hookups and cabins are available as well. Open May through September. ($$)

SHOPPING

Explore Deadwood and you'll find food, jewelry, antiques and souvenirs. Walk old Main Street to explore the offerings in town. Other shops are off Main Street along another busy nearby road, Sherman Street.

CHUBBY CHIPMUNK HAND-DIPPED CHOCOLATES

(420 Cliff St. ☎ 605.722.2447 🖱 chubbychipmunk.net) Located on the outer edge of Deadwood on the road to Lead is this chocolate-lover's haven. Chubby Chipmunk is a good place to fill a small bag of handmade chocolates and other treats to munch on during the day's travels. There are many flavors, like favorites butter cream, toffee and raspberry. Additionally, house specials have fun names like "Hot Mama," a dark chocolate truffle with habañero, jalapeño and cayenne peppers. There's also white chocolate Key Lime and Lemon Meringue. This little shop was featured on an episode of Every Day with Rachel Ray, and it had a three-page write-up in The Chocolate Travel Guide. Shop owners travel to national chocolate conventions, and recently won several awards including a first place for their Moose Toffee Truffle at the Seattle Chocolate Salon. ($)

ANTIQUE EMPORIUM

(409 Cliff St. ☎ 605.717.1646 🖱 deadwoodantiques.com) Collectors walk this sprawling 10,000-square-foot rustic store that houses thousands of items, from antiques and old advertising memorabilia to rummage-sale fare. There's lots to explore in various nooks and crannies jammed with items ranging from taxidermy moose heads and old green jars to

Deadwood

coins and political buttons from past campaigns. Check out their online store to see a sampling of goods.

CASINO RESTAURANTS

Walk into the casinos along Main Street to see historic woodwork and furnishings above and between the slot machines. Ornate woodwork, stained-glass windows and brass trim refer back to Old West days. If gambling is not your thing, you can enjoy one of the many restaurants. Menus are available to review the offerings and prices before you commit to taking a seat.

Casino establishments in Deadwood are generally not family-friendly, so check with the restaurant before making your visit if you have children. (Some of these casinos also have hotels, see the "Hotels" section for more information).

MIDNIGHT STAR ✪ Must See!

(677 Main St. ☎ 605.578.1555 ⚓ themidnightstar.com) Midnight Star features a comfortable bar, casino and two restaurants in a historic downtown Deadwood building, owned and extensively remodeled by Kevin Costner. Plexiglas cases with actual costumes, props, and memorabilia from his movie career are scattered throughout the complex. One case has his *Field of Dreams* movie baseball jersey, and another holds a *Waterworld* wardrobe item. Many more movie posters, photos of Costner in movies, and actual costumes and props from his films fill the Midnight Star.

On the second level is Diamond Lil's Bar and Grill, where the food is good and reasonably priced. And there's also top-notch fine dining in a plush setting available at the vastly more expensive Jake's on the top floor. At Jake's, international cuisine is lavishly served by an attentive staff and an award-winning chef. It has the best collection of wine in the Black Hills. ($/$$$)

THE LODGE AT DEADWOOD

(100 Pine Crest Ln. ☎ 605.584.4800 🖰 deadwoodlodge.com)
A newer facility in Deadwood is located just north of town on Highway 85, at the top of a hill. There are two restaurants here: The Deadwood Grille and Oggie's Sports Bar & Emporium. Both use the same kitchen, but the bar side is less expensive and less formal than the fine-dining section. It's a comfortable place, and the service is prompt and friendly. The sports side has pool tables, darts, and 10 high-definition flat-screen televisions are tuned in for nonstop sports action. The more formal side, with a warm, elegant feel, features fine-dining dishes paired with private-label wines. It's part of a top-notch hotel facility with an elaborate pool for guests, and a spacious Las Vegas-style casino plus more than 260 machines.

CADILLAC JACK'S

(360 Main St. ☎ 866.332.3966 🖰 cadillacjacksgaming.com) The dining room at Cadillac Jack's is rather plain, but good for a quick bite with the family. Jack's serves breakfast, lunch and dinner as well as offering a full service bar, with appetizers and specialty coffees. It features homemade soups, steak, sandwiches and cheesecake. The restaurant is next to the casino, but separated by a large entry so it's still family-friendly. Cadillac Jack's is adjacent to an AmericInn hotel, and guests of the hotel can have room service delivered from the restaurant. ($)

Deadwood

DEADWOOD GULCH RESORT & GAMING

(304 Cliff St. ☎ 605.578.1294 🖱 deadwoodgulch.com) The restaurant at Deadwood Gulch has a homey atmosphere and made-from-scratch dishes. The restaurant is in a building separate from the main hotel, but on the same grounds. Hotel guests get free breakfast, a choice from several fresh cooked-to-order sit-down offerings—a nice alternative to some accommodations that have only cold donuts or other self-serve breakfast areas. The restaurant has added bakery and fudge-shop offerings, treats made on site for sale from large glass cases at the restaurant entry. Recommended by locals. ($)

SILVERADO FRANKLIN

(709 Main St. ☎ 605.578.3650 🖱 silveradocasino.com) The all-you-can-eat Friday and Saturday night buffet features crab legs, baked fish, crawfish, prime rib, vegetables, soup and salad bar, bread sticks and dessert. Silverado Franklin also offers breakfast and lunch buffets. There's a soup and salad bar buffet open for lunch Monday through Saturday, featuring prime rib and ham, broasted chicken and fresh veggies. The slow-roasted prime rib is soft and tasty, and stars most any time of day including on the Saturday breakfast buffet along with eggs, bacon, sausage and biscuits and gravy. There's also a Sunday brunch. It's an interesting setting in this historic hotel, with an adjacent gaming complex. ($$)

SALOON NO. 10 / DEADWOOD SOCIAL CLUB

(600 Main St. ☎ 605.578.1944 🖱 saloon10.com) During your walk down historic Main Street, stop into the bar where Wild Bill Hickok was shot and killed, while holding the famed "dead man's hand" of aces and eights. The actual site is a storefront across the street, but the "new" No. 10 has been there since the 1930s. It's still a bar today, with the added features of a ground floor casino and a restaurant upstairs called the Deadwood Social Club. Kids are welcome to come with parents to watch a reenactment of the shooting of Wild Bill until about 8:30 p.m.

The bar is a rustic place with sawdust on the floor. It has a comfortable, museum-like atmosphere with antiques, old pictures and historic Western and mining-camp artifacts spanning more than 100 years. It even has Wild Bill's chair that he supposedly was sitting in when shot. Food served upstairs in the 19th century-decorated restaurant is consistently good, with many Italian dishes. There's an extensive wine list, and an outdoor rooftop bar next to the restaurant.

The desserts have won awards, and include cheesecake flavors like butter-brickle with caramel sauce, and mocha chocolate chip with chocolate sauce. The place is usually jumping with card tournaments, actors recreating the shooting of Hickok several times each afternoon, and both local and nationally known bands performing. ($$)

OTHER RESTAURANTS

Of course, you don't have to go through a casino to grab a bite to eat in Deadwood. There are several choice places in town that don't try to seduce you with the flashing lights and noise of a casino floor.

Deadwood

DEADWOOD THYMES CAFE & BISTRO

(87 Sherman St. ☎ 605.578.7566) Deadwood Thymes is a secluded getaway a few blocks east of the noisier Main Street strip of casinos and restaurants. It's a great break from the casino food fare. While the menu seems to change a lot, the food quality remains top notch. It's a cozy place with a good wine list. Lots of locals eat here among the wrought-iron chairs and Old World paintings. Hours may vary, so call ahead. It's usually closed on Mondays, and after lunch and some evenings. Check out the desserts, including a killer pineapple upside down cake.

There are plenty of meat dishes, but folks who don't eat meat will find some unique choices. For example, there's a muenster cheese and Greek olive sandwich on a whole-grain bread, served with a dried tomato spread and baby lettuce, and on the side a deli pickle, chips and a piece of orange. Nice offerings. ($$)

BOONDOCKS

(21559 US Hwy 385, 9 miles south of Deadwood ☎ 605.578.1186 🖰 fiftiesfun.com) Watch for the Ferris wheel and other carnival rides that help you find this 1950s rock 'n' roll-themed diner. This place features burgers, malts, homemade fries and classic cars. Open May to October. ($)

HOTELS

It's mostly casino accommodations in this town, but that's why many come to Deadwood. Sleep where you play, play where you eat, eat near the machines. Take a walk along Main Street to get a feel for the place—there are many casino hotels from which to choose. Others are scattered around the fringes of town for those who don't want to stay directly in the party zone.

DEADWOOD GULCH RESORT & GAMING

(304 Cliff St. ☎ 605.578.1294 ⬤ deadwoodgulch.com) Visitors often return to this hotel located away from the main strip of casinos. It has a variety of gaming machines and tables in its own casino area. Free snacks are available in the late afternoon. Take a break on the outdoor patio facing a small, winding creek and forested hill. There's access to the water for folks who like to get their feet wet. Rooms are clean, quiet and offer basic amenities.

If you are coming to gamble, sign up for a member card. Each month features different promotions and games, promo give-aways, VIP parties and more. Random players are selected for extra bonuses including free pulls on several machines. ($$)

COMFORT INN GULCHES OF FUN

(225 Cliff St. ☎ 605.578.7550 ⬤ gulchesoffun.com) There is an on-site amusement park at this hotel and casino, giving the kids something to do in this city long on casinos. There's 18-hole mini-golf, a NASCAR go-kart track, bumper boats with squirters, a small train, a large arcade and a few rides for the very young. There's a full casino, too. The hotel has free high-speed Internet access, continental breakfast with coffee and weekday newspaper. Also on site is an indoor heated pool, hot tub and exercise room. Deluxe suites have a microwave and refrigerator. If you play enough, points earned can be spent on cash back, meals, clothing, hotel rooms and day passes to the amusement park. ($$)

Deadwood

CELEBRITY HOTEL

(629 Main St. ☎ 605.578.1909 ☗ celebritycasinos.com) Recently restored, there's also an auto museum at this downtown hotel. Rooms have antique-looking furniture, big televisions and heated towels. There's a minimal breakfast: free packaged goods like breakfast burritos in the refrigerator. The free museum has many cars, such as James Bond's Aston Martin, Magnum P.I.'s 308 Ferrari, a jeep from *MASH*, one of Evel Knievel's jump bikes, and props from 75 movies including Terminator 2.

It's a little strange to enter through the casino and check in at the cashier's window. But once you get upstairs the place has a nice feel. Touches like heated towels and high-quality soaps (better than those little bars found in lower-budget hotels) give it a classy feel. In the downstairs casino, after 5 p.m., there are often free hotdogs and fresh buns—a nice perk for players. ($$)

MINERAL PALACE HOTEL AND GAMING

(601 Main St. ☎ 605.578.2036 ☗ mineralpalace.com) Opened in 1993, this 75-unit hotel includes the Gem Steakhouse and Saloon, three casinos, a liquor store and gift shop. It's downtown where parking is very hard to find, so access for guests includes a private parking area and elevator for a secure feeling. There are king-size beds, robes, in-room hot tubs, refrigerator and large flat-screen televisions in suites that offer both hardwired and wireless Internet. Granite tubs, showers and vanities are found throughout. VIP suites have balconies and fireplaces. In 1876, entrepreneur Al Swearengen arrived in rowdy Deadwood, and a year later he established the Gem Theatre on the site now occupied by the Mineral Palace. There was entertainment, including a house of prostitution. ($$/$$$)

BED & BREAKFASTS

More than a "like home" experience, these bed and breakfasts have perks to make you want to settle in. Each one is different, off in the forest but not too far from Deadwood's offerings, without having to stay in the middle of the downtown casino hotels.

BLACK HILLS HIDEAWAY BED & BREAKFAST

(Just off Hwy 385, 7 miles south of Deadwood ☎ 605.578.3054
☗ enetis.net/~hideaway) This is a mountain chalet-style house with eight large rooms, all with private baths. There are cathedral ceilings above a natural-wood interior, a huge brick fireplace and deck. The inn is located on a former wagon trail used during the late 19th century. It's situated on 67 acres, with hiking and biking on the premises—complimentary mountain bikes are available for guests. A full hot breakfast is served from 7 to 9 a.m. in the dining room or on the deck. Box lunches are available for trips or hiking, at an extra charge. No pets. ($$)

STRAWBERRY BED & BREAKFAST

(21291 Strawberry Hill Ln. ☎ 605.578.2149
☗ strawberrybnb.com) The Strawberry is located three miles south of Deadwood on Highway 385. There are full bathrooms and individual entrances, great views, and both feather and non-feather beds. Two large hot tubs are on either end of the cabins. A full country-style breakfast is included, with

waffles, spiced pears and apples, bacon, ham or sausage, juice and coffee, fresh brewed tea, hot chocolate or a beverage of your choice. ($/$$)

CAMPING

Campers have a couple of places to stay right in town, but most campgrounds are outside of town, among the rolling landscape and evergreens of the Black Hills.

DAYS OF '76 MUSEUM & CAMP

(17 Crescent St. ☎ 605.578.2872 🖱 daysof76.com) Nestled on the banks of Whitewood Creek, fishermen here tell of good luck catching trout. The trolley to downtown Deadwood stops at this campground for folks who need a lift to the shops, casinos, restaurants and saloons. This is an RV park, with 30 full hookup sites, a gift shop, showers and a dump station.

WHISTLER GULCH CAMPGROUND

(235 Cliff St. ☎ 605.578.2092 🖱 whistlergulch.com) This campground and RV park is on a wooded hill at the edge of Deadwood, in the southwest corner of town. The city's trolley makes regular rounds and boards at the front door of the lodge. There's a heated swimming pool on site, as well as a shower house and laundry facility. The lodge store has grocery items and RV supplies.

FISH 'N FRY CAMPGROUND

(5 miles south of Deadwood on Hwy 385 ☎ 605.578.2150 🖱 fishnfry.com) Living up to its name, trout fishing is allowed without license or limit, and the staff will cook the fish you catch. This 50-year-old campground also has ATV and off-road trails near the property, so riders don't need to use a trailer to take equipment to paths. There are 60 campsites, wireless Internet access, and sites near restrooms, showers, heated swimming pool and a recreation area. There also are three cabins available for rent that hold two to seven people. A grocery store, gift shop and laundry are on site, as well as a café.

MYSTIC HILLS CAMPGROUND

(21766 Custer Peak Rd. 10 miles south of Deadwood
☎ **605.584.4713** 🖰 **mystichillscampground.com)** In addition to standard campsites, Mystic Hills has cabin rentals and motor home spots with full and electric-only hookups. Tent sites are available, as well as long-term full hookup campsites. A café on the grounds offers charbroiled steaks, pork chops, fish, shrimp, beer, wine and more. There's a convenience store with basic food and camping supplies.

ROUBAIX LAKE

(About 14 miles south of Deadwood on US Hwy 385
☎ **605.642.4622)** Campers can scout out sites along four loops through the pine trees located here at the Roubaix Lake campgrounds. It's one of few campgrounds in the Black Hills National Forest with a beach and wheelchair-accessible toilets. There are more than 53 tent sites, but no RV sites or boat ramp. Motorboats not permitted on this lake. The fishing is good though, because the lake is stocked with rainbow trout.

Deadwood

Want to learn more about Deadwood's history, attractions, casinos, and hotels?

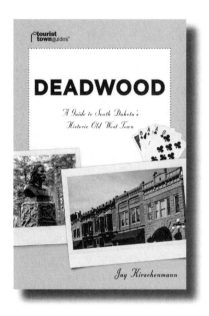

Deadwood: A Guide to South Dakota's Historic Old West Town

by Jay Kirschenmann

For Details Visit:

http://www.touristtown.com

Sturgis and Piedmont

For 70 years, the northeastern Black Hills town of Sturgis has been host to the world-famous Motorcycle Rally, which, in recent years draws thousands of people during a few weeks each summer.

The town's history goes back before the age of partying bikers to its founding in 1876. It was named after Major Samuel D. Sturgis, a commander at the nearby Fort Meade Cavalry Post, located on the eastern edge of town.

The fort served as a U.S. Cavalry post to nearly every cavalry regiment in the U.S. Army. Soldiers trained at the fort and served in several wars. Today people come to the area primarily for the rally. Otherwise, there's not a lot to do in this sleepy little town of about 7,000, beyond enjoyment of the natural surroundings, including nearby Bear Butte State Park.

Folks tired of driving themselves have several options in Sturgis. There are several taxi services, including **Ace Taxi** *(1939 Davenport St.* ☎ *605.720.8294),* **Courtesy Taxi** *(*☎ *605.347.4253),* **Party Bus & Taxi** *(13326 Barry Lane* ☎ *605.206.0128)* and the **Hot Springs Night Owl Taxi** *(2142 Minnekahta Ave.* ☎ *605.745.7550).*

For general information about Sturgis, contact the **Sturgis Chamber of Commerce and Visitors Bureau** *(2040 Junction Ave.* ☎ *605.347.2556* 🖱 *sturgis-sd.org and the city's* 🖱 *sturgis-sd.gov).*

ATTRACTIONS

The world-famous Motorcycle Rally is king for a few weeks in August, but there are other things to do, including checking out bikes from decades past at the local motorcycle museum. A sacred mountain is nearby, open to the public but special to Native Americans.

BEAR BUTTE STATE PARK ✪ Must See!

(East Hwy 79 ☎ 605.347.5240 ⚲ sdgfp.info/Parks) Bear Butte, eight miles east of Sturgis, features a mountain sacred to many Native Americans who still come to hold religious ceremonies throughout the year. Stop into the Bear Butte Education Center to learn about the history of the mountain.

Artifacts dating back 10,000 years have been found near Bear Butte. In more recent times, tribes continue a spiritual bond with the mountain. Visitors are asked to not disturb colorful pieces of cloth and small bundles or pouches hanging from the trees. The prayer cloths and tobacco ties represent prayers offered by Native Americans during their worship, and should be left undisturbed.

Park officials say that notable Native American leaders have come to the site, including Red Cloud, Crazy Horse and Sitting Bull. Leaders from many Native American nations met to discuss the advancement of white settlers into the Black Hills.

State literature reports that George A. Custer, who led an expedition of 1,000 soldiers into the region, camped near the mountain. Custer verified the rumors of gold in the Black Hills, and Bear Butte then served as a visual landmark that helped guide the rush of invading prospectors and settlers toward the Hills.

Today's visitors fish in Bear Butte Lake, hike around the water or up Summit Trail, camp and horseback ride. A buffalo herd roams the base of the butte, but park rangers warn that the animals are wild and should not be approached. The park has earned national distinctions, including being placed on the National Register of Historic Places in 1973, and declared a National Natural Landmark and a National Historic Landmark. Summit Trail is a designated National Recreation Trail. ($)

STURGIS MOTORCYCLE RALLY

(☎ 605.720.0800 ☗ sturgismotorcyclerally.com) For a few weeks each year in August, this small town at the northeast edge of the Black Hills is packed with thousands of people on motorcycles. Sturgis is transformed to biker haven during the annual Sturgis Motorcycle Rally. But the big bikes don't just stay in this tiny town. Riders love to tour the Hills, so the natural sound of birds and streams are replaced, for a time, with the throaty rumble of motorcycles.

Visitors can join the party of thousands with music concerts by local and national bands, lots of drinking and visits by celebrities. Others may choose to avoid the Black Hills entirely during the week when bikers rule, and most hotels hike their rates. The event seems to get bigger each summer, and the thousands of bikers fill hotels in cities throughout the Hills. Specific dates for rallies are outlined on the website.

STURGIS MUSTANG RALLY

(🖱 sturgismustangrally.com) More than just motorcyclists book time in Sturgis too: Mustang car fans have their own weeklong celebration. The car show and races usually are held during the last week of August or first week in September each year.

MOTORCYCLE MUSEUM AND HALL OF FAME

(999 Main St. ☎ 605.347.2001 🖱 sturgismuseum.com) This interesting museum of vintage and unusual motorcycles is located in the former post office building on the corner of Main Street and Junction Avenue. Appropriate for the bike-gathering capitol, the Motorcycle Museum is a showplace for rare, unusual cycles and scooters dating from the early 1900s to the present. From 1930s-era Harley-Davidsons and Sears-brand cycles made in the '60s, to makes including Lewis, Douglas and Ace, bike fans find lots to admire here. There are two levels of displays in this attraction that has been listed as one of the 1,000 Places to See Before You Die by author Patricia Schultz. ($)

ACCOMMODATIONS

There are a few motels in town, but be sure to book Motorcycle Rally weeks far in advance. That goes for Sturgis and the rest of the Black Hills during rally days.

HOLIDAY INN EXPRESS HOTEL & SUITES

(2721 Lazelle St. ☎ 605.347.4140 🖱 hiexpress.com) This Holiday Inn Express is a fairly new hotel, located just off the highway. It has a game room, fitness center and heated indoor pool with a hot tub and water slide. There's a free hot breakfast for guests that features pretty darn good cinnamon rolls. The hotel offers a free shuttle into nearby Deadwood or to the Rapid City Regional Airport. ($$)

DAYS END RV PARK

(Interstate 90, Ext. 30, East side of the Interstate, 2501 Avalanche Rd. ☎ 605.490.1702/605.347.2331 🖱 daysendcampground.com) There's a convenience store onsite with groceries, laundry, showers and shaded tent camping. Days End is located in downtown area of Sturgis, walking distance from fast food, stores and Main Street. There are 15 very small cabins recently built on the site. ($)

LEGENDS B&B AND LOG CABIN SUITES

(20809 Legends Ln. 1 mile east of Deadwood, just off 14A ☎ 605.578.2780 🖱 blackhills.com/legends) The four cabins at Legends Bed & Breakfast are billed as a romantic hideaway, including The Bordello Rose Suite that depicts an early brothel in historic Deadwood. Others are themed, too, like the Oriental Suite that has furnishings that recall the Chinese culture in Deadwood during the late 1800s. The cabins include soft robes, books, magazines and romantic games. ($$)

PIEDMONT ATTRACTIONS

Incorporated in 2007, the town between Sturgis and Rapid City is situated where the Black Hills rise abruptly from the Red Valley. It's officially a newly incorporated town, but Piedmont has records of residents since the railroad came through in the 1800s. The town gets its name from French words pied ("foot") and mont ("mountain"). There's not a lot here, but a few stops may interest travelers.

PETRIFIED FOREST OF THE BLACK HILLS

(I-90 Exit 46, 8228 Elk Creek Rd. ☎ 605.787.4884
🖱 elkcreek.org) Visitors take a self-guided tour to see petrified trees that are 38 to 130 million years old. These rocks and prehistoric fossils are scattered in a walk-through area along a several blocks. The staff is friendly and knowledgeable. The stone logs vary from five to 100 feet in length, and three to five feet in diameter. Rock stumps start at about three feet high. There's a rock shop next to an RV park with camping cabins and a heated pool. ($)

WONDERLAND CAVE

(☎ 650.578.1728 🖱 southdakotacaves.com/wonderland) It's a scenic drive off Interstate 90 to find this tourist attraction that opened in 1929. Find it by taking Exit 32 at Sturgis, follow the signs along Vanocker Canyon Road. Inside this cave are a wide variety of formations—walls and ceilings covered with stalactites, flowstone, popcorn crystal, and helictites. Walking trails and a restaurant are also on the grounds. Cave tours, which leave about every 20 minutes, are offered May through October. The guides are friendly and know and share their knowledge of cave geology. It's a leisurely pace, and the temperature always is 47 degrees, so a light coat or sweatshirt is recommended. Be sure to wear comfortable walking shoes. ($)

Attractions in Central Black Hills

Some Black Hills attractions are often in towns, but many more in this region are scattered in between the towns. The center of the Black Hills is where some of the most famous attractions are found, including the mountain carving **Crazy Horse National Memorial.**

Getting to any of these attractions is half the fun. Remember that travel time can sometimes be several hours. Plan your driving time, perhaps by creating an itinerary for various day trips. Bring along some snacks and drinks for the road.

CRAZY HORSE MEMORIAL

(12151 Ave. of the Chiefs ☎ 605.673.4681 ● crazyhorse.org)
Located along U.S. Highway 16/385, about 17 miles southwest of Mount Rushmore and just north of Custer, Crazy Horse is an immense, ongoing mountain carving project with no set completion date. The face of the Native American chief honored by the sculpture is finished, and the horse's head is starting to take shape. The late sculptor Korczak Ziolkowski's widow, Ruth, and many of their sons and daughters are usually at the site, carrying on his work.

Visitors sometimes see drilling and blasts on the mountain. When finished, the monument will stand 563 feet tall—nearly 10 times the height of Mount Rushmore. Unlike Rushmore, it's planned to be a full sculpture in the round. Visitors can spend at least a couple of hours at the memorial's visitors complex. There's a 40,000-square-foot welcome center and theaters, the Indian Museum of North America, the Native American Educational & Cultural Center, the sculptor's original log house studio and workshop, indoor and outdoor galleries, a museum gift shop, restaurant and snack bar areas and an expansive viewing veranda.

June 2008 marked the 60th anniversary of the first blast on the mountain, and the 10th anniversary of the dedication of Crazy Horse's completed face. Open May through September, the "Legends in Light" show starts at dark. The memorial may be open during winter months; contact them in advance. ($)

REPTILE GARDENS ✪ Must See!

(6 miles south of Rapid City, on Hwy 16 ☎ 605.342.5873 🖱 reptilegardens.com) Family-owned since 1937, Reptile Gardens is a popular indoor attraction. Living up to its name, there are alligators, crocodiles, snakes, frogs and lizards on display, as well as colorful parrots, hawks, owls and falcons. Rock hounds will find displays of minerals and prehistoric fossils, and plant lovers will spend time examining all the botanical specimens throughout the attraction.

Expect to walk a lot at this attraction, but seated shows featuring demonstrations by animal handlers are also part of the experience. Galapagos and Aldabra tortoises munch on grass and veggies, including the 500-pound Methuselah, who is nearly 130 years old. Maniac the crocodile still lives here, too, impressive when he's on the move at more than 15 feet long and more than 1,000 pounds. The attraction won awards over the years, and was listed in the *USA Today* "Top 10 Places in the U.S. to Stop the Car and Take a Look." Open April 1 to December 31. ($)

BEAR COUNTRY U.S.A.

(13820 S. Hwy 16, 8 miles south of Rapid City ☎ 605.343.2290 ⬤ bearcountryusa.com) While it's called Bear Country, this drive-through nature preserve is home to more than 25 different species of animals, from timber wolves, mountain lion, buffalo, and Rocky Mountain goats, to Dall sheep, big-horn sheep, elk, and waterfowl. Visitors stay in their "cages" (your vehicle) while driving through the 200-acre attraction. The animals roam free.

A section called Babyland is a quarter-mile loop with waterfalls, where visitors walk to see dozens of species of smaller animals live. Playful bear cubs are a popular stop halfway through the loop. A shuttle service is available in this section. The Bear's Den, a 6,000-square-foot gift shop, is filled with wildlife-theme items geared toward folks who love animals, nature and the great outdoors.

Ice cream, cold drinks and treats are available at the snack shop, but there's also a picnic area for folks who bring along their own lunch. Since it opened in 1972, Bear Country has been a traditional stop for visitors to the Black Hills. Open from late April to late November. ($)

COSMOS MYSTERY AREA

(24040 Cosmos Rd. ☎ 605.343.9802/605.343.7278 ⬤ cosmosmysteryarea.com) There's something odd going on at Cosmos Mystery Area: people stand at a strange angle in some areas, balls roll uphill, and visitors feel an unusual pull of gravity. The trick is obvious, and this attraction has many like it around the country. But if you're a fan of "optical illusion houses," this is an interesting diversion. The leaning effect is entertaining for adults and kids. The optical illusions are amusing.

Cosmos is an enjoyable stop that has brought the more-than-50-year-old attraction national attention in magazines and on television shows. Children age 11 and under get in free. Hot dogs (100 percent turkey), corn dogs, sloppy Joes and other snacks are available. There's not much walking required during the half-hour guided tour at this attraction, located just northeast of Mount Rushmore. Families open to having fun get a lot of laughs out of this stop, for three generations now. Open April through October. ($)

THUNDERHEAD UNDERGROUND FALLS
(10940 W. Hwy 44 ☎ 605.343.0081 🖱 thunderheadfalls.com)

Thunderhead is one of the oldest gold mines open to the public in the Black Hills. Visitors take an easy self-guided 600-foot walk inside the mine. In 1878 gold miners blasted into the canyon wall letting tons of icy water loose into the gold mining tunnel. At eight cubic feet per second, it's still running today. It's a passive attraction, owned and operated by the Harold Johnson family who says they intend to keep the area as natural as possible. There's no gift shop or outside distractions—just the natural beauty of the canyon in which it nestles.

Gold-bearing quartz veins and living stalactites are clearly visible throughout the tunnel. The drill marks that carved out the tunnel over 125 years ago can still be seen. Thunderhead is open daylight hours, May to November. ($)

BLACK HILLS CAVERNS

(2600 Cavern Rd. ☎ 605.343.0542 📞 blackhillscaverns.com)
Compared to other area national park caves that sprawl for miles, Black Hills Caverns is small. It is also privately owned, and the guides make it a personal cave-visiting experience. There's an easy half-hour, 1,500-foot walking tour of one level, with lots of calcite crystals. A harder, three-quarter-mile complete tour takes about an hour, and goes through all three levels of the cave. It's a moderate hike. Visitors see frost crystal, amethyst, logomites, calcite crystals and others. ($)

SITTING BULL CRYSTAL CAVERNS

(13745 S. Hwy 16, 9 miles south of Rapid City ☎ 605.342.2777 📞 sittingbullcrystalcave.com) The Sitting Bull Crystal Caverns features a 40-minute tour that involves lots of stairs. The very young or getting older may not like the nearly 200 steep steps. With a history dating back to a cooperative effort with area Native Americans, the attraction still carries some authentic tribal art and crafts, along with lots of modern tourist items, in the gift shop. It also carries a wide selection of books about Native American culture. The grandson of the original 1929 owners, Alex and Mamie Duhamel, still runs the attraction. ($)

CRYSTAL CAVE PARK

(7770 Cave Rd., Hwy 44 West ☎ 605.342.8008) While a little pricey for a tour that sometimes can get crowded, this is one of the least strenuous tours of its type in the area, in one of the region's smallest commercial caves. Tours last about 40 minutes with several stops, as the guide tells about a variety of formations, including six-point crystals, stalagmites and hailstone spar crystals. ($$)

PUTZ N GLO

(23694 Strato Rim Rd. ☎ 605.716.1230 🖱 putznglo.com)
Located two miles southwest of Bear Country on Highway 16,
Putz n Glo is an indoor, black light, rock 'n' roll-themed mini-
golf course. ($)

THE RANCH AMUSEMENT PARK

(6303 S. Hwy 16, 3 miles south of Rapid City ☎ 605.342.3321
🖱 **ranchamusementpark.com)** There's a lot to do at The Ranch
for fans of amusement parks, including go-karts, a 25-foot-tall
rock climbing wall, water bumper boats, an 18-hole miniature
golf course and a big video arcade. Drinks, hot dogs and pizza
are available. ($)

OLD MACDONALD'S PETTING FARM

(9 miles south of Rapid City on Hwy 16 ☎ 605.737.4815
🖱 **oldmacsfarm.blackhills.com)** Old MacDonald's Petting Farm is
a favorite stop in the Hills for young children. It's a clean place
with more than 100 animals to pet, including bottle-feeding
baby goats, lambs and calves. Pig races run five times each day,
and there are pony rides as well. Animals are calm and tame.
For people in the area for a few days, the admission price is
good for three consecutive days. The staff is helpful and cour-
teous. ($)

FORT HAYS CHUCKWAGON SUPPER AND SHOW

(4 miles south of Rapid City on Hwy 16 ☎ 605.394.9653
🖱 **mountrushmoretours.com)** You can get a bit of the Old West
feel with this cowboy supper and old-timey music. The food is
good, and the entertainment will amuse those who like folksy
Western music. There's also an all-you-can-eat breakfast. A

Sylvan Lake *(© Jay Kirschenmann)*

Badlands National Park *(© Jay Kirschenmann)*

The Mammoth Site *(© Jay Kirschenmann)*

Deadwood Streetlight *(© Jay Kirschenmann)*

Wild Bill Hickok's Grave (© *Jay Kirschenmann*)

Downtown Keystone *(© Jay Kirschenmann)*

Spearfish Canyon *(© Jay Kirschenmann)*

Pactola Reservoir *(© Jay Kirschenmann)*

Needles Highway *(© Jay Kirschenmann)*

Rushmore Cave *(© Jay Kirschenmann)*

Wall Drug *(© Jay Kirschenmann)*

Mount Rushmore and Avenue of the Flags (© iStockphoto.com/ blackestockphoto)

portion of the movie set from *Dances with Wolves* is on display. There's more to see along the boardwalk, too, including turn-of-the-19th-century storefronts including a tin shop, rope shop, blacksmith and sawmill. ($)

PACTOLA RESERVOIR

(Between Lead and Hill City on US Hwy 385 ☎ 605.574.4402) Located 11 miles north of Hill City, the Pactola Reservoir is a beautiful lake and surrounding natural forest, a favorite stop when traveling U.S. Highway 385. Travelers can't miss it since the highway crosses the top of the dam for a half-mile, offering great views of the lake. Pactola was created in the late 1950s by the dam on Rapid Creek, about 15 miles west of Rapid City. It is named for the site of the former town of Pactola, a site that is now at the bottom of the lake.

Hike on the scenic overlooks, bring a snack for the picnic grounds, or stay longer using the campgrounds and boat ramps. Fishing is plentiful because the lake is stocked with rainbow trout, brown trout and perch. Open year-round, there's a small visitors center here too, and a nearby commercial boat rental business. Camping sites are in three loops, with many walk-in tent sites between mature pines. Some sites overlook the lake .

PACTOLA PINES MARINA

(23060 Custer Gulch Rd., Pactola Reservoir ☎ 605.343.4283 ☝ pactolapines.com) Groups can rent a pontoon boat for half-day or whole-day trips on the lake. One pontoon rental has a slide to the water built on deck. For a less expensive outing there are also small boats and canoes available for rent to get out on this beautiful lake. The marina offers a "lunch on the water" feature, a nice service for a reasonable fee. Boaters call or stop by to tell the staff the time they want lunch, then float in to pick up the prepacked picnic. It includes plates, napkins and forks. There's a new large cabin available for rent, too, nestled back on a forest hill .

SHERIDAN LAKE

(Just north of Hill City, just off Hwy 385 and County Rd. 228
☎ **605.343.1567)** Sheridan Lake is a good place for sightseeing and perhaps for having a picnic at this mirror-like, clear moun-tain lake. The lake has beaches, campsites, hiking trails and picnic areas. The Sheridan Lake Marina has boat rentals, bait and tackle, boat launching facilities, and camping and fishing supplies. The town of Sheridan used to be here, but during the Great Depression the federal government dammed Spring Creek at the north end of town, and the Civilian Conservation Corps created the lake. Today fishermen report catching lots of yellow perch, northern pike, largemouth bass and trout.

The south side of the lake has a campground with five loops, some overlooking the lake. The shore has several places where boats can be tied up near camping sites. The campground is spread out along Sheridan Lake on pine-covered hillsides. Grassy sites are spacious and widely spaced. Interpretive programs are given at the amphitheater several evenings during the summer.

SHERIDAN LAKE MARINA

(16451 Sheridan Lake Rd. ☎ 605.574.2169
🖰 **sheridanlakemarina.com)** There are inexpensive non-motor-ized rentals of kayaks, canoes and pedal boats here, but parents must accompany children. If you want to motor around on

the lake, the marina rents pontoon boats and small aluminum fishing boats. There's a minimum rental charge for up to two hours. An hourly rate is charged after the two-hour mark, with discounts for morning and evening blocks, and all-day rentals.

Visitors find lots of supplies here, too, for camping and fishing, firewood, grocery items and swimming accessories. There are horseshoe pits in the front of the building, and inside, aquariums are filled with each type of fish that is stocked in the lake.

DEERFIELD LAKE RESERVOIR

(About 20 miles west of Hill City on Forest Service Rd. 17 ☎ 605.343.1567) A 10-mile trail leads around Deerfield Lake for hiking, bicycling, horseback riding and cross-country skiing. The campground, one of three in the Deerfield Recreation Area, is located on Deerfield Lake. All tent sites are walk-in with good privacy, have excellent views of the lake and located in a heavy stand of Ponderosa pines. The RV sites are in the open, on the lake, and don't have much privacy. There are no RV hookups, but dumping stations are available.

Getting to Deerfield Lake is half the fun: the drive on Forest Service Road 417 to the campground is through the 8,000-acre Reynolds Prairie. It's a pleasant summer drive from Hill City to the lake, with glimpses of antelope and grouse, and lots of wildflowers. Horses are allowed on Forest Service land, both open range and on the trail. There's no swimming beach at this lake.

DEERFIELD LAKE RESORT

(11321 Gillette Prairie Rd. ☎ 605.574.2636

▟ deerfieldlakeresort.com) Tent camping, RV electric or full
hookups and cabins are on this lake west of Hill City on
Forest Service Road 17. There are laundry and shower facilities on site. No dogs are allowed, but this resort does have a
horse camp with a corral and barn. Snowmobilers, ATV riders
and both fishing and hunting guests also stay here. Canoe,
4-wheeler and snowmobile rentals are available. Hunters say
the resort is a home base for some of the best elk, turkey and
deer hunting in the Black Hills.

HORSETHIEF LAKE

(Just west of Keystone on State Hwy 244) Two miles from
Mount Rushmore, the National Forest campgrounds have two
loops—one for RVs and tents and the other for tents only.
Some sites overlook the lake among pines and large boulders.
There are seven walk-in tent sites. Ice and soft drinks are avail-
able at the gatehouse.

Hill City

★

Hill City, a town of about 900 in the central Black Hills, is home to the 1880 Train, which runs along the original railroad bed between old mining camps along the way from Hills City to Keystone. The town has a quaint downtown strip of shops along both sides of Main Street. They are filled with art galleries, gift shops, eating establishments and more.

The town began back in the old days with only a few residents who built shacks, and several who lived in tents when the gold rush started in 1876. After the rush died down, stagecoaches and the railroad kept the city going.

The world took notice of Hill City and its Black Hills Institute of Geological Research when news agencies covered the discovery of "Sue," the most complete Tyrannosaurus Rex specimen ever found. The saga of Sue involved confiscation of the skeleton, lawsuits and the famous auction at Sotheby's that sold the T-Rex for $8.3 million to Chicago's Field Museum of Natural History. The institute has its own museum where visitors can see many examples from the Jurassic period found in this region.

For general information about Hill City, contact the **Hill City Chamber of Commerce** *(324 Main St.* ☎ *605.574.2368* 🖱 *hillcitysd.com).*

ATTRACTIONS

Hill City is a very small town, but is packed with dozens of shops along Main Street. Stroll along the wide, concrete walks decorated with old-fashioned streetlights and explore some of the storefronts.

JON CRANE GALLERY

(256 Main St. ☎ 605.574.4440 ⬤ joncranewatercolors.com)
Among the shops along Main Street is the sales gallery and studio of watercolor artist Jon Crane. He has a traditional, realistic painting style and often likes to show subjects he finds in the region: old buildings, abandoned country homes, barns, farms and landscapes.

The artist lives nearby, and sometimes can be found in the gallery or nearby, working on a painting or sketch of a prairie or mountain scene. Original watercolors, limited edition giclee and lithograph prints, open-edition miniatures and note cards are available for sale.

MUSEUM OF NATURAL HISTORY ✪ Must See!

(117 Main St. ☎ 605.574.4505 ⬤ bhmnh.org) Dinosaur exhibits are abundant at the museum, both real fossils and skeletons, as well as exhibits cast from the real thing. The museum shows off many of the best area finds including fossilized fish, mammals, reptiles, trilobites and more. The museum is located in a space provided by the **Black Hills Institute of Geological Research** *(⬤ bhigr.com)*, a known leader in paleonto-logical excavations and preparation since 1974.

The Institute supplies museums and collectors with fossils and cast replicas. Their casting of the T-Rex named Stan is at Walt Disney World in Florida. Stan is one of the most studied dinosaurs of all time, with other castings featured in museums throughout the world, including the Smithsonian Institute, the

National Science Museum in Tokyo, the Korea Institute of Geoscience in Daejon, Korea, the University at Oxford in the UK and more than 30 other museums worldwide.

The T-Rex skeleton named Sue was sold to Chicago's Field Museum of Natural History. Excavations of Sue, Stan, Bucky, Duffy and Wyrex are among the top 10 most complete T-Rex skeletons ever discovered. Everything Prehistoric Gift Shoppe has a vast assortment of educational merchandise that reflects museum exhibits. ($)

1880 TRAIN ✪ Must See!
(222 Railroad Ave. Hill City/103 Winter St., Keystone
☎ 605.574.2222 ▮ 1880train.com) The 1880 Train is a real train that takes passengers on a two-hour round trip along an original stretch of track between Hill City and Keystone. It's a picturesque ride through a section of the Black Hills you cannot see by car. Black Hills trains were gone until entrepreneurs and train buffs in the 1950s restored steam-powered locomotives to again make this run between the vintage late 1800s Hill City Depot and Keystone.

The train winds its way through rocky hills and prairies, the actual route that the CB&O Railroad made in the late 1880s to service the mines and mills between the two cities. Locals along the way never tire of waving at people aboard the train, and passengers often take the cue and wave back. Most of the open cars have a roof, and if it rains there are clear plastic window shades that can be pulled down.

The train runs five times a day, from May through the first two weeks of October. There's popcorn for sale for the natural show: deer are often seen on the way, along with horse pastures, mountains, prairies, several old nonworking mines and Harney Peak in the distance to the east. One of several classic engines at the attraction has been in several movies, and in an episode of the 1960s television show Gunsmoke. Round trips are the most popular, but one-way trips are available. ($$$)

PRAIRIE BERRY WINERY

(23837 Hwy 385 ☎ 605.574.3898 🖱 prairieberry.com) Located at the northern edge of Hill City, there's no longer a tour of the winemaking facility at the Prairie Berry Winery. But wine lovers and curious novices alike can stop in for a free wine tasting for an education about each type of wine before selecting a bottle to take home. Hosts have a casual, friendly approach to serving up samples that are made from South Dakota wild grapes and other "prairie berries," some of which are not berries at all.

Some wines have fun names like Red Ass Rhubarb, a tangy, semisweet wine made from rhubarb and red raspberries. Other names and ingredients refer to the region, like the Deadwood, a semi-dry red wine made from piney black currants in the area, Pheasant Reserve, a spicy dry red chokecherry and grape wine aged in oak, named for the state bird. The Frontenac, another semidry, is made from the South Dakota Frontenac grapes.

It's a casual way to explore the range of tastes created by the winery, several which have won awards across the nation and internationally. While the tasting is free, there's also food for sale in a small Euro-deli tucked in the back corner. The deli has sandwiches, soups and salads, and imported aged cheeses. You can buy wine here by the glass or bottle. There are nonalcoholic drinks as well. The business is open year-round and the location offers you a view of Harney Peak from the patio seating. It's a family-run business, the fifth generation now making wine in South Dakota.

WADE'S GOLD MILL MINING MUSEUM
(12401 Deerfield Rd. ☎ 605.574.2680 🖰 wadesgoldmill.com)

Wade's is a rustic-looking attraction about three-quarters of a mile from Hill City. It features restored mining equipment, a modern placer mill in operation, panning lessons for visitors and a gift shop. The guided tour is just over an hour. ($)

MISTLETOE RANCH
(23835 Hwy 385 ☎ 605.574.4197 🖰 mistletoeranch.com)

Mistletoe is not a ranch at all—the two-story vintage house just north of Hill City on U.S. Highway 385 is a year-round Christmas store. It's a large store, filled with decorations, ornaments and fully trimmed trees. The house used to be located 10 miles farther north, in the former town of Pactola (now at the bottom of **Pactola Lake**). With the construction of the dam and resulting lake in 1958, the town's buildings were relocated throughout the region.

DINING

There are several places to eat, despite Hill City's small size. The Alpine Inn should be your first choice. If you're in a hurry, there are chains serving sandwiches at the **Amoco Food Shop** *(700 Main St.)* or the **Dairy Queen** *(373 Main St.)*. Hike around to see several other offerings.

BUMPIN' BUFFALO BAR & GRILL

(245 Main St. ☎ 605.574.4100 🖱 bumpinbuffalollc.com) This 100-year-old bar serves food, simple home-style cooking, with some local specialties like buffalo burger and chislic, a South Dakota specialty of cubed meat, usually beef, tossed into a deep fryer. It has a clean, relaxed atmosphere, and looks like a spot where locals come to meet friends, and where families eat. ($)

ALPINE INN ✪ Must See!

(133 Main St. ☎ 605.574.2749 🖱 alpineinnhillcity.com) The historic 1886 building that houses Alpine Inn has a big, open-air front porch, and inside a lot of reasonably priced, above-average-quality dishes to choose from. Food styles are ethnic European as well as contemporary. Patrons stop in to eat, or sometimes for a drink and try some of the 30 homemade desserts. Favorites from the 11 a.m. to 2:30 p.m. lunch menu are dumplings, pork chops, bratwurst, soups and fresh salads. The 5 to 10 p.m. evening choice is simple: the only thing on the menu is filet mignon, two sizes, served with a lettuce wedge, house dressing, baked potato and Texas toast.

There's a warm atmosphere here, a comfortable feel and great food for travelers along U.S. Highway 385. Started by Waldtraut "Wally" Matush after she moved to the United States from Stuttgart, Germany in the 1960s, her family and several long-time employees continue the traditions and attention to quality she started.

Alpine Inn is a hotel as well. All upstairs hotel rooms are nonsmoking. The hotel and restaurant do not take credit cards, but checks are accepted. Open all year, Monday through Saturday. ($)

DESPERADOS COWBOY RESTAURANT

(301 Main St. ☎ 605.574.2959) Not a bad place for a quick bite to eat. The log walls date back to 1885. Try the buffalo burger and sweet potato fries, and catch it on the right day for great homemade soups. It has a Western atmosphere—an interesting dish is the Cowboy Spaghetti and cornbread. Open every day for lunch during the afternoon, and supper during the evenings. ($)

HOTELS

If this little town grows on you, it may be the Black Hills destination you're looking for to stay for a night or two. Being in the central Black Hills, it's a quick trip to destinations both north and south. There are a few options, in town and nearby.

COMFORT INN

(616 Main St. ☎ 605.574.2100) Comfort Inn is a clean, well-maintained hotel. It offers comfortable beds, and some rooms are large and with hot tubs. A gas station, convenience store and sandwich shop are located next door. This chain offers free continental breakfast with make-your-own waffles, but no elevator to the second floor. Deer sometimes can be seen grazing in the field behind this hotel. ($$)

LODE STONE MOTEL AND CABINS

(23884 Hwy 385 ☎ 605.574.2347 🖱 blackhills.com/lodestone) At Lode Stone, guests can choose between cabins or standard motel-style rooms. The small, rustic log cabins sleep four people (look out the back window and see a stream). They have private baths, kitchens with stove, refrigerators, microwaves and cookware, and television. There are common front porches where guests often visit. The motel rooms are small; some have microwaves and refrigerators. These rooms sleep about two to four people. ($)

MOUNTAIN VIEW LODGE

(12654 S. Hwy 16 ☎ 605.574.2236 🖰 mountainviewlodge.net) Located at the junction of Highways 16 and 385, the cabins at Mountain View are available in different sizes and sleep from four to eight people. There are also standard motel rooms, with a small swimming pool and hot tub on site. Lots of knotty pine walls give the place a warm feel. The motel has family units with two bedrooms, which have oak furnishings and wall prints from a local Native American artist. One cabin has a master bedroom on the first level along with a kitchen furnished with a small fridge, coffee pot, microwave, oven, dishes and table. There is a futon in the very small living area, with a television mounted high. Upstairs is a small loft with bunk beds, and another small room with a double bed. The cabin is clean, but there's not much storage space for clothes. There's a gas grill on the deck. ($$)

SPRING CREEK INN

(23900 Hwy 385 ☎ 605.574.2591 🖰 springcreekinn.com) Spring Creek Inn is located on three and a half acres just north of Hill City. Grounds include basketball, volleyball, playground equipment and a stream. There is also a picnic shelter with gas grills. Most evenings a fire roars in the open fireplace and guests are invited to visit. Larger A-frame lodges can be booked for bigger groups or families. ($$)

ALPINE INN LODGING

(138 Main St. ☎ 605.574.2749 🖱 alpineinnhillcity.com) All the rooms have queen-size, pillow-top beds and down comforters in this historic building, home to the best restaurant in the region. Along with a vintage look to the ornate wooden bed frames and décor, there are modern features including coffeemakers and blow dryers in each room. All have updated bathrooms, although room No. 3's bathroom is directly across the hall from the room. It's a small hotel, and old, but is nicely kept. All rooms are air conditioned and have ceiling fans. Some say it's home to friendly ghosts that roam the main hall. ($$)

GOLDEN SPIKE INN AND SUITES

(601 E. Main St. ☎ 605.574.2577) Built in 2005, this Best Western hotel has luxury family suites with full kitchens. Also available are budget family rooms, special rooms with fireplace and Jacuzzi, executive suites, as well as standard guest rooms. There's an indoor pool, hot tub, fitness center, and an outdoor heated pool. There's an on-site restaurant, gift shop and laundry too. ($/$$).

NEWTON FORK RANCH

(12407 Deerfield Rd. ☎ 605.574.2220 🖱 newtonforkranch.com) Thee fully furnished vacation cabins are available year-round for nightly or weekly rentals. The Mickelson Trail runs through the property for hikers, bikers and horseback riding. There are no horses for rent here but guests are welcome to bring their own. It's a restful hideaway hosted by Linda Flounders, third-generation owner. Modern, spacious cabins nestle into the trees, with full decks and lots of windows. Deer often graze in the meadow, some cabins have fireplaces, and without city lights the night sky is a sparkling free light show above. See inside and outside pictures of the cabins online. ($$)

BED & BREAKFASTS

Most bed and breakfasts are outside Hill City, except for the **Mountains to Prairie**. The establishments' websites offer pictures of the accommodations for people to see prior to making the drive; a little time online could be worth the homework.

MOUNTAINS TO PRAIRIE B&B
(200 E. Main St. ☎ 605.574.2424
🖱 mountainstoprairiesbb.com) Mountains to Prairie offers rustic wood-beamed accommodations with modern furnishings in two suites. Upstairs is the Log Accented Suite with a hand-crafted log stairway. The Knotty Pine Cabin-Style Suite is on the ground level—the master bed is made of local Ponderosa pine. Mountains to Prairie is located a short walking distance to the shops that line downtown Hill City. ($$)

COUNTRY MANOR BED AND BREAKFAST
(2 miles north of Hill City on Hwy 16/385 ☎ 605.574.2196)
Country Manor is located beside a small stream on sparsely landscaped grounds at Stone Faces Winery. Accommodations are in a manor house, and include a family suite and four standard rooms. Light breakfast is served: fruit, muffins, juice and coffee. ($$$)

DEERVIEW BED & BREAKFAST

(5 miles west of Hill City on Deerfield Rd. ☎ 605.574.4204 🖱 deerviewbb.com) Deerview features cottages in a natural setting. The seasonal establishment operates from May 1 to October 31 and requires a three-day minimum stay. There is a separate cleaning fee. Weekly and monthly rentals are available. ($$)

EMERALD PINES BED & BREAKFAST

(23836 Emerald Pines Dr., 3 miles from Hill City ☎ 605.574.4462 🖱 emeraldpinesrefuge.com) Secluded in a mountain setting, Emerald Pines is a log home, quiet and secluded, with an excellent view. Two suites include a refrigerator, private baths and satellite television. The property features contemporary and antique furnishings, large wraparound deck, and is located on seven acres. Gas grill and picnic table available. Two-night minimum stay required, smoke-free indoors, no pets, adults only. ($$)

HOLLY HOUSE BED & BREAKFAST

(23852 Hwy 385 ☎ 605.574.4246 🖱 bbonline.com/sd/hollyhouse) Located about a half mile from Mistletoe Ranch, there are several themed suites at Holly House: Bridal Suite, Victorian Room, USA Room, Western/ Indian Wolf Room and the Harley-NASCAR room. Another suite is the Christmas Cabin, in the backyard by the stream. Most suites come with jetted tubs. ($$)

COYOTE BLUES VILLAGE BED & BREAKFAST

(23165 Horseman's Ranch Rd. ☎ 605.574.4477 🖱 coyotebluesvillage.com) Owners Christine and Hanspeter (Hans) Streich from Switzerland designed this very large B&B

to resemble a Swiss chalet, a change from those Western and Victorian establishments. Located about seven miles north of Hill City on Highway 385, three floors of rooms are available, many with individual outdoor patios and hot tubs. A European breakfast is served at 8:30 a.m. sharp, or you miss it! Breakfast includes breads, orange juice, tea, eggs, coffee, fresh fruit and Swiss muesli. It's a quiet setting in this central Black Hills location, with easy access to many attractions. ($$)

CAMPING

There are several campgrounds in the Hill City region offering the full gamut of RV sites, trailer spots, cabins and plenty of tent-camping grounds.

CROOKED CREEK RESORTS CAMPGROUND
(24184 S. Hwy 16 ☎ 605.574.2418 🖱 crookedcreeksd.com)
Crooked Creek is a clean, well-organized campground, on 11 acres with lots of shade. There are RV sites, creek-side tenting, modern and rustic cabins, and a motel. The grounds are adjacent to the **Mickelson Trail** for quick hikes or longer treks. Car and bicycle rentals, and a coin laundry are available. Also on the grounds are a smaller outdoor heated pool and kids' playground, and a store with groceries, firewood, propane and more. The highway is adjacent, and can get a little loud, so campers may want to choose sites farther away from the road. Bathrooms and showers have been recently updated.

DEERFIELD LAKE RESORT AND CAMPGROUND
(11321 Gillette Prairie Rd. ☎ 605.574.2636
🖱 deerfieldlakeresort.com) Tent space, RV spots, and modern

cabins are at Deerfield Lake, and most sites have fireplaces. Facilities range from primitive campsites to full hookups with electric, water, and sewer. There's a shower house and laundry facilities. Deerfield also has a horse camp with corrals, set next to 350 miles of groomed and marked trails. There's also access to biking, fishing, hiking, and hunting. If you don't want to bring your own equipment, there are snowmobile, canoe and four-wheeler rentals available.

HORSE THIEF CAMPGROUND AND RV RESORT

(24391 Hwy 87 ☎ 605.574.2668 🖱 horsethief.com) Horse Thief Campground is heavily forested, with fire rings and tables at each site, and wood for purchase. There are cabins, electrical hookups for RVs, and horse camping sites. Extras include a playground, pool, volleyball, basketball, and horseshoe areas, and a store with gifts and snacks. Wireless Internet access is also available. Family owned and operated, the staff is quick to respond to needs and questions. A lot of families stay here on large campsites.

RAFTER J-BAR RANCH

(12325 Rafter J-Bar Rd. ☎ 605.574.2527 🖱 rafterj.com) Located about three miles south of Hill City on Highways 16/385, there's full-time camp security at Rafter J-Bar, with RV, tent, pop-up camper and cabin accommodations. The grounds are made up of five camping areas separated by alpine meadows and shaded by large Ponderosa pines. Choose a remote site, or camp close to the resort's activity center. There are electric, water and sewer sites along with many tent sites. There's a pancake breakfast available, and a nice biking trail on the edge of the property.

Guests can use the free hot showers at three bathhouses. Wireless Internet is available, and some sites have satellite television hookups. A huge, colorful "Earthscapes Structures" kids' playground is on the grounds, along with an arcade and recreation room. A horse-drawn wagon ride and chuckwagon dinner event is available.

TIMBER LODGE RETREATS AND RV PARK
(23821 Hwy 385 ☎ 605.574.4546 🖱 timberlodgeretreats.com)
This company's main business is property management. Many houses and cabins of all sizes, from rustic to luxury accommodations, are available for various lengths of time, and guests are required to sign a rental agreement. There is a booking fee charged for each property based on the size of the rental. Some of the upscale properties also require the purchase of a damage protection plan. The company also offers various vacation packages and concierge services available for the major attractions, ski rentals, snowmobiles and ATV use.

Most properties come with amenities like linens and outdoor grills, and kitchen supplies including stove, refrigerator, coffee pot, toaster, microwave, dishes and basic cookware. ($/$$$)

Keystone

★

The closest city to the **Mount Rushmore** memorial is essentially a strip of tourist shops on each side of the main drag, a few restaurants and several motels. But the place makes a fun visit, popping in and out of various storefronts, and sampling from the many gift shops.

Like other Black Hills towns, Keystone has a history in gold. As mining boomed in the surrounding hills, in 1891 a group of miners started the Keystone Mine. They named the new town that emerged after the mine was operating. It grew slowly until a ledge of gold-bearing quartz was found in 1894. Then mining boomed, busted, boomed again, and huge fires virtually destroyed the business district several times in the early 1900s.

The carving of nearby Mount Rushmore started in 1927, and the town began its rise to tourist town fame. The production of quartz is still a viable industry in Keystone, and the lumber industry continues to contribute to the local economy. But tourism is the biggest industry today. Winter Street is now referred to as The Strip, with businesses on both sides of U.S. Highway 16A leading to Mount Rushmore.

For general information about Keystone, contact the **Keystone Chamber of Commerce** *(110 Swanzey St.* ☎ *605.666.4896* 🖱 *keystonechamber.com).*

MOUNT RUSHMORE AND OTHER ATTRACTIONS

The nearby world-famous Mount Rushmore carving dominates the attractions in this part of the Black Hills. But there are other options, from a presidential wax museum, gold mines, an aerial tramway, and mountain slide. Spend some time exploring the region to find what catches your interest.

MOUNT RUSHMORE NATIONAL MEMORIAL ✪ Must See!
(13000 State Hwy 244, just west of Keystone ☏ 605.574.2523 🖱 nps.gov/moru) If there's a single, top destination within the thousands of acres of trees, rock outcroppings, and lakes within the Black Hills National Forest, it's Mount Rushmore, an iconic symbol of America known around the world. There's no admission fee to gaze up at the massive work by sculptor Gutzon Borglum and his crews, who carved busts of four United States presidents, George Washington, Thomas Jefferson, Theodore Roosevelt and Abraham Lincoln, into the granite mountain. There is a $10 parking fee, good for one year.

About three miles west of Keystone, there's a lot to do here, so allow about two hours for your visit. It's an easy walk from adjacent parking areas to the pedestrian-friendly Avenue of Flags, the observation deck, sculptor's studio and bookstore, restaurant, gift shop and hiking trails. The evening lighting ceremony features a dim-to-fully-lit program that illuminates the huge mountain sculpture accompanied by music and narration. There also are interpretive activities, a half-mile Presidential Trail hike and a look at summer sculptor-in-residence demonstrations.

The 60-foot-high faces, 500 feet up, look out over a forest of pine, spruce, aspen, and birch. There is a large observation deck to view the mountain sculptures, and an open-air theater facing the mountain for ranger-hosted talks. The Mount

Rushmore Audio Tour, a national award winner, tells visitors the story of the area through music, narration, interviews, historic recordings and sound effects while you take a walk around the park. You can rent an audio tour wand for $5 at the Audio Tour Building during the summer season (or at the Information Center during the winter season) and experience an educational, fun and engaging presentation. It is available in German, Spanish, and Lakota. Visitors can either sit down and listen to every entry on the wand or follow a suggested route around the park. A map is provided, but you can choose to make the various stops in any order.

The idea to carve huge figures of American heroes in the Black Hills was conceived by South Dakota state historian Doane Robinson in 1923. He gained support from state leaders and from Washington, D.C. The sculptor, Gutzon Borglum, first looked at the Needles spires Robinson suggested, to see if they could be carved into tall granite figures, but the rock formations were too thin and weathered. Borglum liked Mount Rushmore because it faced southeast and would be well lit most of the day, the National Park Service reports.

The work began on October 4, 1927. Washington's figure was started first, his head carved in a rounded shape with details of the face added later, and dedicated on July 4, 1934. Jefferson was started on Washington's right, but after about two years of work the granite was found to be cracked and unstable, so the beginning of his carving was blasted from the mountain and re-started on the left side of Washington. Jefferson was dedicated in 1936. Abraham Lincoln was dedicated on September 17, 1937, and Theodore Roosevelt's figure in 1939.

For two more years Borglum continued to add details, but in March 1941 he died suddenly of an embolism. Although his son, Lincoln, continued the work for seven months, funding ran out and the sculpture was declared completed. Much of the rubble remains at the foot of the mountain, the result of 14 years of careful blasting with dynamite to remove 450,000 tons of rock, ending on October 31, 1941.

Because the monument is carved in hard, solid granite, the sculpture could easily still look good in 10,000 years and actually could last 100,000, even 200,000 years, according to a scientist quoted on a *History Channel* special.

The Lincoln Borglum Museum & Bookstore and the Sculptor's Studio & Bookstore offer a lot of materials for visitors to take home for further study of the monument. Interpretive activities run during summer months as well as a sculptor-in-residence program. A large concession and dining facility is on the grounds. Hikers can take the half-mile Presidential Trail—the first quarter-mile is wheelchair accessible. It offers spectacular close-up views of the faces. Beyond the accessible section, the rest of the trail is strenuous.

Visit the memorial anytime, 24 hours a day, year-round. The information center is open from daily during the summer (late May through early September) closing near dusk during the winter (October through April). National Park Service staff members give a 10-minute talk followed by a 20-minute film that lasts until after sunset, followed by an impressive slow illumination of the monument with background music, Memorial Day through Labor Day.

To get to Mount Rushmore from Rapid City, drivers on Interstate 90 should take Exit 57 and travel south on State Highway 16 to 16-A through the town of Keystone, to State Road 244. Follow the signs. From the south, follow U.S. Highway 385 north through Hot Springs or U.S. Highway 18 to State Highway 89 north to State Road 244, and follow the signs. There is a $10 parking fee, but no admission fee.

BIG THUNDER GOLD MINE ✪ Must See!

(☎ 605.666.4847 🖥 bigthundermine.com) Big Thunder Gold Mine is an authentic, well-preserved 1890s-era gold mine. They hand out a few free ore samples with the tour, and have one of the largest displays of original mining equipment in the Black Hills area. Gold panning lessons are offered in a trough just outside the attraction, which built next to Battle Creek where gold originally was found on historic Reed's Placer Claim during the 1880s. The attraction has been featured on The *History Channel*. Two gift shops, a restaurant and an ice cream parlor make for a relaxing pause in the action. Open May to October. ($)

TRAMWAY: PRESIDENT'S ALPINE SLIDE AND RUSHMORE TRAMWAY

(☎ 605.666.4478 🖥 presidentsslide.com) It's a pleasant ride to the top of the mountain on a chairlift, and then visitors have a choice of taking the lift back to the bottom or riding down on a slide. These smooth, built-into-the-ground slide trails are 2,000 feet long. Riders control the speed of their individual sleds, and small children may ride with adults. The cautious can take it slow to look at the beautiful terrain, or go at a faster pace to feel the dips and high-banked turns. The chairlift is a high, open ride up through rugged rocks and Ponderosa pines, with a unique view of Mount Rushmore at the top.

There's a park up there, and a restaurant with an open-air deck for cheeseburgers, ice cream and other food. There are a few short hiking trails up here, too, with excellent views, flowers, a stream and little waterfalls. Take the tram back down, or zip down on the slides. Packages include chairlift ride only round trip, or the lift up and slide down. Kids age four through teens seem to love this attraction, some saying it was one of their favorite stops on the trip to the Black Hills. It's a fun ride for adults too. Open late May to early September. ($)

NATIONAL PRESIDENTIAL WAX MUSEUM

(☎ 605.666.4455 ☗ presidentialwaxmuseum.com) This is a history lesson in the nation's democracy told through a narration system, with visual aides that include life-size wax figures of key presidents of the United States. Many are in settings of historic moments, including President Bush after 9/11. There are historical artifacts here too. Next door is a restaurant and the adjacent Holy Terror Mini Golf. Packages can be purchased to see all three attractions.

Parents looking to add some educational exposure to the family's trip to the Hills will like this attraction. Visitors get a glimpse into the nation's past with life-like settings based on historical events. Students can gather information about U.S. presidents through activities designed to interact with the museum's exhibits. Self-guided or museum-guided tours are available. ($)

BORGLUM HISTORICAL CENTER

(☎ 605.666.4448 📱 rushmoreborglum.com) The Borglum
Historical Center tells visitors about Gutzon Borglum (sculptor
of Mount Rushmore), his family and the famous people who
were his friends. A 20-minute film shows blasting on the
mountain during the construction of Mount Rushmore. Stand
next to an exact replica of a full-sized carved eye of Lincoln
to get a feel for the scale of the real carving. Allow about 45
minutes for the self-guided audio tour. ($)

BLACK HILLS GLASS BLOWERS

(909 Old Hill City Rd. ☎ 605.666.4542
📱 blackhillsglassblowers.com) An artist-owned-and-operated
glass studio, visitors can watch artists make blown-glass pieces.
The showroom is filled with one-of-a-kind creations made by
Peter Hopkins and Gail Damin. Using 2,000 degree ovens,
visitors watch as the artists form liquid glass into colorful vases,
bowls, eggs, animals, ships, caketops and more. The blowing
times vary. The finished pieces are for sale. Free admission.

KEYSTONE HISTORICAL MUSEUM

(410 3rd St. ☎ 605.255.5280
📱 keystonechamber.com/kahs/museum.html) The Keystone
Historical Museum is housed in the old Keystone Schoolhouse
building. Built in 1900 and featuring Victorian architecture,
it served as Keystone's full-time school until 1988. Today it
houses mining tools, historic pictures and photo collections,
rock and mineral collections, and historic displays including
Carrie Ingalls memorabilia. The sister of Laura Ingalls Wilder
of *Little House on the Prairie* fame, Carrie moved to Keystone
in 1911, where she lived for 36 years. Also available is The

Old Town Walking Tour. Follow the numbered signs and read about the history of one of the fastest-growing boom towns in the Hills. There are 19 stations on the walking tour, each with a sign describing the location. ($)

BEAUTIFUL RUSHMORE CAVE
(13622 Hwy 40 ☎ 605.255.4384

🖱 beautifulrushmorecave.com) The cave is located between Keystone and Hermosa at Highway 79. From downtown Keystone, turn east at the only traffic light. Follow Highway 40 for six miles to the main entrance. Beautiful Rushmore Cave is loaded with stalactites. A one-hour tour has lots of steps and some narrow areas as the trail winds through a series of rooms and passages. The "Big Room" has thousands of stalactites, stalagmites, ribbons, helictites and columns. Guided tours leave every 20 minutes or so. ($$)

DINING

There's a good restaurant within the Mount Rushmore complex, but there are other offerings in the Keystone area, including lodges, steakhouses and even an Old West chuckwagon dinner that features cowboy music.

CARVERS CAFÉ
(Mount Rushmore ☎ 605.574.2515) Feeding the family while
visiting Mount Rushmore is easy in a food-court style cafeteria. Food ranges from a quick espresso and fresh cinnamon buns to a full-course meal. Décor includes a view of Mount Rushmore—on the terrace or indoors near large windows. An expansive fireplace is made of South Dakota slate.

Breakfasts are inexpensive, and other meal selections are comparable to in-town prices but offer a wider selection, ranging from pot roast, natural beef or buffalo burgers, herb-roasted chicken, homemade soups and buffalo stew chili. There are vegetarian choices as well. An adjacent 5,300-square-foot gift shop is loaded with books and other items , and cases of Black Hills Gold jewelry. ($/$$)

K BAR S LODGE RESTAURANT

(434 Old Hill City Rd. ☎ 605.666.4545 🖱 kbarslodge.com) The K Bar S hotel, about a half mile northwest of Keystone on Old Hill City Road (Highway 40), offers a full restaurant, recommended for home-style meals. The buffalo stew is a regional treat. Also available are prime rib, barbecue pork loin and lemon pepper chicken. A light lunch is a chicken Caesar salad with fresh baked bread. Homemade desserts are on the menu too. The open-feeling high wooden ceiling and finished wood-planked walls give this an upscale yet rustic feel. ($$)

POWDER HOUSE STEAKHOUSE

(24125 Hwy 16A ☎ 650.666.4646 🖱 powderhouselodge.com) Visitors and locals recommend the Powder House. It has earned a national reputation for its prime rib. Buffalo dishes also are served, including fall-off-the-bone barbecue buffalo short ribs, slow cooked for more than 13 hours in homemade sauce. About 40 kinds of wine are available here. You can also eat light with sandwiches and other offerings. ($/$$)

RUBY HOUSE RESTAURANT

(124 Winter St. ☎ 605.666.4404 🖱 historicrubyhouse.com) Some folks come here more for the saloon and the atmosphere than the food, although there is a separate dining room. Cowboy actors on the street call out to potential customers, and inside features fancy, Old West, Victorian-style decorations. There are daily "Comedy Western Gunfights" at the bar, and nightly entertainment.

A large covered front porch runs along the entire length of the building, stocked with tables and chairs for outdoor dining and drinking while keeping an eye on Keystone's main drag. Domestic and import beers are on tap and in bottles. One of the largest antique gun collections on display in the Black Hills is here. You may also be able to meet seven-foot, two-inch-tall Big Dave Murra, a three-time world champion comedy gun spinner. ($/$$)

CIRCLE B CHUCKWAGON

(15 miles west of Rapid City/17 miles north of Hill City, 22735 Hwy 385 ☎ 605.348.7358 ☗ circle-b-ranch.com) Eat at Circle B and see cowboy music shows, or stay longer for a horse trail ride. The main area is built like an Old West town, complete with wooden sidewalks. Woodcarver Doug Ladd is usually working on site. Food includes roast beef, roast buffalo, barbecue chicken with sides served on a tin plate in a covered barn. Kids like the petting corral and playground. Reservations requested, open nightly except Sundays from Memorial Day weekend through mid-September. ($$$)

EXECUTIVE ORDER GRILL

(☎ 605.666.4478 ☗ presidentialwaxmuseum.com) Located next door to the National Presidential Wax Museum and the Holy Terror Mini Golf Course, this is an inexpensive place to grab a burger or other dishes. There's dining outdoors on a spacious shaded patio or in the enclosed dining room. Visitors can watch their meals prepared over an open flame grill. ($)

PEGGY'S PLACE

(434 Hwy 16A ☎ 605.666.4445) Fluffy pancakes and their special recipe for biscuits and gravy are good morning offerings here, and fans of chicken fried steak will like that dish as well. A somewhat limited menu, but sometimes Peggy herself, the owner, will wait on tables. ($)

HOTELS

The mountain carving spurred growth of a wide range of motels, hotels, and lodges in this region. Some like waking up to being close to the memorial and so many other central Black Hills attractions. Accommodations cover a range of choices, from budget to luxury rooms.

BEST WESTERN FOUR PRESIDENTS LODGE

(24075 Hwy 16A, near Keystone ☎ 605.666.4472
🖱 **bestwestern.com)** This is a clean, nice-looking hotel in a natural location up against a wooded hillside. There is a two-story natural stone fireplace in the lobby area, and an open stairway to the second floor built with area rough-cut lumber. Offers a good breakfast including some hot dishes. Indoor pool and exercise room are on site. ($$$)

ECONO LODGE OF MT. RUSHMORE MEMORIAL

(908 Madill St., State Road 40 E. ☎ 605.666.4417
🖱 **econolodge.com)** A little off the strip, in a back neighborhood, this motel offers quite small but affordable rooms, and

always seems clean. Visitors saving money for attractions who don't need lots of other amenities may be well served here. A light breakfast of toast, English muffins, some mini muffins, breads, apple juice, coffee, and soft-boiled eggs is included. There is also a spacious, attractive indoor pool. ($)

HOLIDAY INN EXPRESS HOTEL AND SUITES

(321 Swanzey St. ☎ 605.666.4925 🖰 ichotelsgroup.com) This Holiday Inn is recommended for being clean and quiet. It's an easy walk to the main strip downtown. Complimentary breakfast includes biscuits and gravy, bacon and eggs, and cinnamon rolls, but the eating area is very small. Plan on taking your food outside or back to your room. Wet bar, refrigerator and microwave in rooms are handy additions. ($$$)

K BAR S LODGE

(434 Old Hill City Rd. ☎ 605.666.4545 🖰 kbarslodge.com) You can see a profile of George Washington off in the distance on nearby Mount Rushmore from some rooms, some room decks and from the grounds of K Bar S. There are well-stocked breakfast offerings, from omelets to biscuits and gravy (alternating days), and more. There is, however, no pool. ($$)

POWDER HOUSE LODGE

(Hwy 16A ☎ 650.666.4646 🖰 powderhouselodge.com) Powder House offers both log cabin and motel-style lodging. The cabins are tucked in among trees and hills around the grounds for a private feel, but it does make for some steep drives or walks, and tight parking. There are about 40 rooms here, including deluxe family cabins that sleep six. A honeymoon suite has a private hot tub. Public patio and heated outdoor pool and kids' playground also are on the grounds. The motel has no elevator, so if you don't want to climb the stairs on the side of the building, ask for a ground-level room. Open May through September. There is also an excellent restaurant here. ($/$$)

RUSHMORE EXPRESS

(320 Old Cemetery Rd. ☎ 605.666.4483 🖱 rushmoreexpress.com)
The nicer suites have a granite fireplace and wet bar in the living room, Starbucks coffee with the coffeemaker and goody bags. There are heated floors, fogless mirrors and two plasma televisions in the rooms. But as nice as the hotel is, there is a helicopter pad across the street, so it can get a little noisy some days. Interior corridor entry suites are nicer and have less smoke smell than the outside corridor older rooms, which haven't been updated in a while. A continental breakfast of coffee, juice, milk, toast, bagels, pastries and yogurt is swamped by guests each morning in high season. ($$)

BED & BREAKFASTS

Some of the offerings near Keystone follow a theme for each room. Some welcome families and offer to help plan your day trips, while others cater to adults only.

ANCHORAGE BED & BREAKFAST

(24110 Leaky Valley Rd. ☎ 605.574.4740 🖱 anchoragebb.com)
At Anchorage, vacationers will find four nautically themed rooms with private baths, fireplaces, and satellite televisions. King- and queen-size beds, free wireless Internet, and hot tubs under the stars are part of the amenities. Specialty meals can

be provided, and the facility is wheelchair accessible. Guests usually can see wildlife from balconies, decks and porches. Evening snacks are served in the living room where a grand piano and a game table are available. Rooms are decorated around nautical American author themes. ($/$$)

BUFFALO ROCK LODGE

(24524 Playhouse Rd., 2 miles from the entrance to Custer State Park ☎ 605.666.4781 🖥 buffalorock.net) Buffalo Rock is a huge, newer log-beamed structure with wood floors and Western, Native American and "antique" furnishings. Long-time Black Hills residents Art and Marilyn Oakes offer three rooms: one sleeps a couple and the others from four to seven people each. There's a whirlpool tub and a big claw-foot tub in one room. Art is known for his signature hash browns and bacon with eggs and fruit in the mornings, as well as raspberry French toast. The couple is available to help plan day trips, including driving instructions. The home has a reading area and pool table section, offering space for guests to spread out. Children age eight and older are welcome. Outside, there's a big porch where wild turkeys regularly come by for handouts. ($$)

ELK RIDGE BED & BREAKFAST

(12741 Matthew Crt. ☎ 605.574.2320) Five miles northeast of Mount Rushmore, this three-room, adult-only bed and breakfast has a huge, green backyard that borders an undeveloped forest. From here guests can see the undisturbed, natural side of Mount Rushmore. All three rooms have Sleep Number beds, private decks and a hot tub. Substantial breakfasts can include pork chops or ham, omelets, maple sausage or bacon, potatoes on most mornings in many forms, biscuits and gravy, fruit, and homemade cornbread. Vegan meals are available on request. ($$)

CAMPING

There are several places to camp in and near Keystone, and if camping near one of the world's largest works of art is your thing, you'll probably want to stake your claim near Keystone.

KEMP'S KAMP

(1022 Old Hill City Rd. ☎ 605.666.4654 🖱 kempskamp.com) Five minutes from Mount Rushmore, this camp is about 1.5 miles west of Keystone on County Road 323. Tent campers will find showers, a heated swimming pool and elevated fire pits. There are also RV sites with full hookups, some creek-side, and fully furnished one- and two-bed cabins. Free wireless Internet access is available.

SPOKANE CREEK CABINS AND CAMPGROUND

(24631 Iron Mountain Rd. ☎ 605.666.4609

🖱 **spokanecreekresort.com)** This family-owned campground and cabin complex on nearly 30 acres has well-shaded sites, and modern cabins ranging from small to large, with full kitchens. It has a fenced-in swimming pool, general store, gas pumps and propane supply. Several lakes and streams are nearby. Make reservations for the **Sturgis Motorcycle Rally** week, but be forewarned, the owners say that this is not a "party" campground.

If there's a single, top destination within the thousands of acres of trees, rock outcroppings and lakes within the Black Hills National Forest, it's Mount Rushmore.

Rapid City

The second-largest city in South Dakota is home to some 67,000 residents, on the central-eastern edge of the Black Hills. It's the largest city in the region, founded in 1876 by a group of disheartened prospectors who showed up in search of gold.

Today there are more than 100 restaurants, ranging from fast food and bagels to fine dining. Shopping is concentrated in the historic downtown area, and the 110-store **Rushmore Mall**. A commercial airport serves the region. The town is geographically divided to the east and west by hills, about a half-hour drive from the **Mount Rushmore National Memorial**, which is just over 23 miles southwest of the city.

The **City View Trolley** gives visitors a narrated tour of businesses and attractions for $1 per rider, less for seniors. The tour starts at **Milo Barber Transportation Center** *(333 Sixth St.)*, winds through downtown Rapid City and continues west to Stavkirke Chapel, from 9:20 a.m. to 6:30 p.m. Monday through Saturday, late spring to early fall. In the summer, bicyclists can ride the 13.5-mile trail along Rapid Creek, or along the wide-shouldered highways.

For information about Rapid City, contact the **Rapid City Area Chamber of Commerce** *(444 Mt. Rushmore Rd.* ☎ *605.343.1744* 🖱 *rapidcitychamber.com)*. You can also contact the **Rapid City Visitor & Convention Bureau** *(*☎ *605.718.8484* 🖱 *visitrapidcity.com)*.

TAXI SERVICES AND CAR RENTALS

Navigating along unfamiliar streets is tough, although GPS systems work well in the city compared to many parts of the Black Hills. If drivers have a hard time finding their way around Rapid City, an option is to grab a cab. There are lots to choose from.

If you want to go out of town, **Rapid Taxi Inc.** *(505 E Watertown St.* ☎ *605.348.2020* 🖱 *rapidtaxi.com)* also offers sightseeing tours, as does **Airport Express Shuttle** *(1720 E. Center St.* ☎ *800.357.9998* 🖱 *rapidshuttle.com)* with some Black Hills tours available.

For in-town travel there's **Dial A Driver** *(1800 Shaver St.* ☎ *605.721.7299),* **Tigers Taxi & Delivery** *(*☎ *605.641.3151)* and **Yellow Cab** *(*☎ *605.645.1757).*

Go in style with **Hess Limousine Inc.** *(*☎ *605.641.3838* 🖱 *hesslimos.com)* and **Presidential Limousine** *(112 N Maple Ave.* ☎ *605.390.3691* 🖱 *5starlimo.com).*

Many car rental offices are located at the city's airport. A few others around town include **Dollar Rapid City Car Rental** *(410 N Cambell St.* ☎ *605.342.7071)* **Enterprise Rent-A-Car** *(110 N. Cambell St.* ☎ *605.399.9939),* **Casey's Auto Rental** *(1318 5th St.* ☎ *605.343.2277),* **Rent-Rite Car Rentals** *(1600 E. Blvd., No. 44* ☎ *605.342.6696)* and **Thrifty Car Rental** *(*☎ *605.393.0663).*

ATTRACTIONS

Rapid City covers a lot of square miles, with the usual movie theaters, fast food and finer dining restaurants, stores and shops found in similar-sized towns across the nation. But it has several unique features, too, worthy of a closer look. It could be a welcome break from days in the wild, undeveloped regions elsewhere in the Black Hills.

STORYBOOK ISLAND

(1301 Sheridan Lake Rd., No. 9196 ☎ 605.342.6357 📱 storybookisland.org) This free attraction lets kids play on statues and recreation equipment made in Humpty Dumpty, Pinocchio, and other storybook-themed characters. The nonprofit attraction is supported by donations (which are not required). Summer events and performances are scheduled nearly every day in the Children's Theater. Open daily May 24 to September 1.

RUSHMORE WATERSLIDE PARK

(1715 Catron Blvd. ☎ 605.348.8962 📱 rushmorewaterslide.com) Easily seen from the main roadway, Rushmore Waterslide Park has 10 slides and heated water. Slide features include high-speed chutes and 400-foot-long twisters. There's a freestyle ramp, and inner tube rides in the River Run. Very young visitors can use the kiddie pool and an oversized hot spa holds dozens of people. Admission covers the entire day, including mini-golf. Swimsuit and towel rentals are available at this 17-acre, fully staffed attraction. Visitors also will find changing rooms, hot showers and lockers, a video arcade and a gift shop. ($$)

BLACK HILLS MAZE FAMILY ADVENTURE PARK

(3 miles south of Rapid City on Hwy 16 ☎ 605.343.5439 📱 blackhillsmaze.com) Kids and adults wander "lost" in this a life-size labyrinth, 1.2 miles of walkways, bridges and towers. There is a cool-off area with water balloon launchers for relief on hot days. Other attractions here include the Maze Mountain, a challenging 360-degree climbing wall, a seated swinging kiddie ride called Roller Racers, a batting cage area, miniature golf, basketball and billiards. The attraction's website has a couple of online maze games for kids, too. ($)

CITY OF PRESIDENTS

(302 Main St. information Center ☎ 605.343.1744 📱 visitrapidcity.com/whattodo/thecityofpresidents) Along Main Street are life-size bronze statues of many U.S. presidents made by South Dakota sculptors. The visitors center, open noon to 9 p.m. Monday through Saturday, June 1 to October 1, contains a history of presidents. The project started in 2000 and continues to add four statues each year.

MUSEUM OF GEOLOGY

(South Dakota School of Mines & Technology at 501 E. St. Joseph St. ☎ 605.394.2467 📱 sdmines.sdsmt.edu/museum) This museum can be an interesting stop for visitors or families who like minerals, fossil specimens, and skeleton displays of giant reptiles, fish and dinosaurs from the ancient seas of South Dakota. It's a free museum on the college campus, and includes recovered meteorites and exhibits of fluorescent minerals. Gold from the area, fossils, rocks and minerals excavated by paleontologists make up nearly 350,000 specimens. It's an educational yet interesting stop that's open year-round.

JOURNEY MUSEUM

(222 New York St. ☎ 605.394.6923 📱 journeymuseum.org) The Journey Museum has a large collection of exhibits from when the Black Hills region was formed during a violent geological upheaval more than 2.5 billion years ago. There's also background and examples from the Western frontier among the major prehistoric and historic collections. Exhibits help visitors understand the area's history from both Native American and European pioneer points of view. Open year-round, free for kids under age 10. ($)

DAHL FINE ARTS CENTER

(713 Seventh St. ☎ 605.394.4101 ☗ thedahl.org) Fans of the arts will find the Dahl's schedule filled with changing art exhibits, musical concerts, theater activities and special events. The center features 200 years of U.S. history with a painted, panoramic mural enhanced by lighting and narration. The art galleries showcase works from regional and national artists. The facility, which opened in 1974, is western South Dakota's largest contemporary visual arts, arts education and performing arts center. It is a public facility owned by the City of Rapid City. ($)

CLEGHORN SPRINGS STATE FISH HATCHERY

(Hwy 44 West ☎ 605.394.4100 ☗ sdgfp.info) Just west of Meadowbrook Golf Course, this fish hatchery even provides food for visitors to feed the fish. It's a working hatchery, on the west end of Rapid City, just off Jackson Blvd., raising and releasing nearly one million rainbow trout and Chinook salmon annually. The hatchery is located at a natural spring that produces about six million gallons of water a day. The Aquatic Education Interpretive Center is on the hatchery grounds. The 1950s-era facility was totally rebuilt in 2007. The visitors center is open Memorial Day to Labor Day, while the aquatic center is open year-round.

DINOSAUR PARK

(940 Skyline Dr., west off Quincy St. ☎ 605.343.8687) For decades visitors have come to the top of Skyline Drive to see seven life-size concrete replicas of dinosaurs that can be seen from most anywhere in Rapid City. Kids enjoy climbing on the dinosaur tails and visitors take pictures of each other. Families can spend perhaps an hour walking among the huge dinosaurs, looking around in the gift shop and buying a few treats at the concession stand. Built in the 1930s, the park offers a great view of Rapid City from atop this high hill. It's a pretty low-key destination, but a nice break from a hectic schedule. The free attraction is open May to October.

FLAGS AND WHEELS INDOOR RACING

(405 12th St., Exit 55 or 57 off Interstate 90 ☎ 605.341.2186 🖱 flagsandwheels.com) Some attractions at this indoor cart racing facility are rather expensive. It's a huge space, about 47,000 square feet near downtown Rapid City. From the outside it has an industrial look, but there's lots to do inside, including paintball, laser tag, bumper cars, slot cars, batting cages and an arcade. Youngsters may get annoyed at the slot cars that are not easily kept on the track. Visitors looking for more of a thrill can try the Biz Carts, which go more than 40 miles per hour on a 27,000-foot track. Flags and Wheels is one of the only facilities in the United States to import these powerful racing carts from England. The fumes can be a little strong in here. Open Tuesday through Sunday. ($/$$)

CHAPEL IN THE HILLS

(3788 Chapel Ln. ☎ 605.342.8281 🖱 chapel-in-the-hills.org) This chapel is a replica of the famous 850-year-old Stavkirke (Stave

Church) in Norway. Inside, a recording tells visitors about the building's architecture, history, symbolism and connection to the Christian church. Open May 1 to September 30, with evening services nightly June through August. Includes a log cabin museum, built by a Norwegian prospector who came to the Black Hills during the gold rush of the late 1800s. Free, but donations are accepted.

MEMORIAL PARK AND BERLIN WALL EXHIBIT

(444 Mount Rushmore Rd. ☎ 605.343.1744) The free exhibit is two 12-foot segments of the actual Berlin Wall, relocated to Memorial Park, next to the Civic Center on Rapid Creek. Photographs and information accompany the exhibit. Paved trails meander through the park and take visitors to a rose garden.

BLACK HILLS COMMUNITY THEATER

(Rushmore Mall, 2200 N. Maple Ave. ☎ 605.394.1786 🖰 bhct.org) An acting troupe, made up of local members of the community, puts on five shows between September and May each year. The group moved into a new facility in 2008, to what they call "Theatre in the Mall," between JC Penney and RadioShack.

THE SOUTH DAKOTA AIR AND SPACE MUSEUM

(Ellsworth Air Force Base, 2890 Davis Dr. ☎ 605.385.5189 🖰 sdairandspacemuseum.com) The South Dakota Air and Space Museum offers bus tours of the base and the Minuteman II missile silo, available mid-May through mid-September for a small fee. There's a charge for the onsite IMAX. The museum and large airpark feature aircraft displays, exhibits inside the hangars and a gift shop. The museum is open seven days a week. Admission is free.

DINING

There are unique dining options offered in Rapid City, from the revamped nearly 100-year-old firehouse to a restaurant that offers local and organic ingredients in its dishes. Of course, there are standard chain restaurants in town as well.

FIREHOUSE BREWING COMPANY

(610 Main St. ☎ 605.348.1915 🖱 firehousebrewing.com) The restaurant and brewery is housed in an original 1915 city firehouse—interesting surroundings for a drink or dinner. The décor is memorabilia from old-time fire halls, including huge wooden ladders that span the ceiling, and polished brass and firefighting equipment that decorate the walls and the bar. The restaurant and lounge are on two floors, and a mostly outdoor patio offers dining and live music during the summer. On the third level is the Firehouse Dinner Theater. Meal quality is consistent, but the various beers made on site are the star attraction. The menu covers a lot of ground, from salads and pasta, to buffalo and gumbo. ($$)

THE CORN EXCHANGE

(727 Main St. ☎ 605.343.5070 🖱 cornexchange.com) The Corn Exchange is a small, 32-seat, fine dining experience several steps above the norm of tourist travel dining. It's a slow-food choice for those who want bistro-style cuisine. The restaurant uses local and organic ingredients when possible in its farm-to-table offerings. Favorites include lamb, filet mignon and pork

Milanese. It's open for dinner Tuesday through Saturday. The menu is suited to adult tastes—many kids probably wouldn't like or appreciate the special dishes served here. It has been featured in *Food Arts, Gourmet*, and *Better Homes & Gardens* magazines as well as in the *New York Times* and the *Washington Post.* ($$$)

SAIGON RESTAURANT

(221 E. North St. ☎ 605.348.8523) Locals say that this is the best restaurant in the region to find Chinese-style, Vietnamese and even some Thai dishes. The food is outstanding, especially its General Chicken, the Lemongrass Chicken, and the Shrimp Fried Rice (ask for double shrimp—you'll be glad). The food is all made to order so it takes a little longer than many places, but it's worth the wait. The staff makes customers feel like part of a family. ($)

TALLY'S

(530 6th St. ☎ 605.342.7621) The beloved but formerly time-worn 1930s-era diner at Sixth and St. Joseph streets in down-town Rapid City was recently remodeled. The new owners reopened it as a modern "fine diner." Old menu items still are served, like hot beef sandwiches, patty melts, pancakes and pie. Gourmet entrees have joined the old offerings, including an excellent beef tenderloin with a coffee-cocoa rub and rhubarb artichoke butter. Wine is sold, including by the glass . ($/$$)

DELMONICO GRILL

(609 Main St. ☎ 605.791.1664 delmonicogrill.biz) Located across from the Firehouse Brewing Co., this is one of Rapid City's more upscale dining venues. Expect to settle in for a couple of hours or more to enjoy a night of dining. American grill cuisine is served in a jazzy atmosphere, with steaks, roasted lobster and slow-cooked prime rib topping the menu. Entrees are multi-course rather than a la carte. There's bread and oil, salad and soup, and an extensive wine and beer list. ($$/$$$)

Rapid City

COLONIAL HOUSE RESTAURANT

(2501 Mount Rushmore Rd. ☎ 605.342.4640) The casual Colonial House restaurant and bar is smoke free. You'll find good food at a good price with excellent service. Homemade caramel rolls are a treat, while buffalo burgers are juicy. Steak and seafood is available, along with barbecue ribs and desserts. ($)

GOLDEN CORRAL

(1180 North Lacrosse St. ☎ 605.399.2195) Open every day, the Golden Corral is a safe bet to please a group of all ages and tastes. It's a buffet that includes home-style favorites, including steaks, shrimp, fried chicken, pot roast, meatloaf and burgers. There also are lots of fresh vegetables and desserts. ($)

GOLDEN PHOENIX

(2421 W. Main St. ☎ 605.348.4195) This restaurant serves both Chinese and Korean dishes. *Rapid City Journal* readers chose it as the "Best Chinese Restaurant" for several years running. ($)

FLYING T CHUCKWAGON SUPPER AND SHOW

(8971 S. Hwy 16 ☎ 605.342.1905 🖰 flyingt.com) Located about six miles south of Rapid City near Reptile Gardens, dinner includes Western music and comedy. ($$/$$$)

ACCOMMODATIONS

There are dozens of motels along the main roads in Rapid City. But there also are landmark hotels, like the Alex Johnson, that stand high on the city's skyline.

HOTEL ALEX JOHNSON

(523 Sixth St. ☎ 605.342.1210 🖱 alexjohnson.com) A prominent fixture in downtown Rapid City, the historic Hotel Alex Johnson, with a Tudor-style top floor exterior, dominates the city's skyline. In 1927 construction began on the hotel, the day before work began on Mount Rushmore. Less than a year later, the first guest registered.

Listed on the National Register of Historic Places, six U.S. presidents have stayed at the Alex Johnson: Calvin Coolidge, Franklin D. Roosevelt, Dwight D. Eisenhower, Richard Nixon, Gerald Ford and Ronald Reagan. It's in the center of town, so dining and shopping areas are within walking distance. While it has a historic look and feel, the hotel has modern amenities including wireless Internet. Pets are allowed in some rooms. There is a fine-dining restaurant on site too.

Check out a live streaming video of downtown Rapid City from the hotel's rooftop webcam, on the hotel website. Take a walk outside behind the hotel to see the block-long "Art Alley," thousands of works of graffiti on exterior walls, dumpsters, poles and any other surface that will hold paint. ($$)

FAIRFIELD INN & SUITES

(1314 N. Elk Vale Rd. ☎ 605.718.9600) Families with children may choose this location for the huge indoor waterpark, but the Fairfield Inn may not be suited to those who don't want lots of children in the halls and crowding the breakfast area. The water attraction isn't included in the nightly rates, although packages are available. It's a 30,000-square-foot indoor water-park with slides, a lazy river, and a 40-game arcade with ticket redemption for prizes. There is a full grill and bar area. ($$)

PEREGRINE POINTE BED & BREAKFAST

(23451 Peregrine Pointe Pl. ☎ 605.388.8378 🖱 peregrinebb.com)
A newer getaway, Peregrine Pointe is located about seven miles southwest of Rapid City, off Sheridan Lake Road (Highway 228). It's in the middle of 15 acres of pristine forest for hiking and bird watching. There's a large common room with a stonewall fireplace, and a side video room with fireplace too. The five large, modern guestrooms are tastefully decorated. A full complimentary breakfast is served in the dining room, out on the deck or in your room. Children age 10 and older are welcome for an additional charge. ($$)

SHOPPING

Like other larger cities, there are endless shopping options. Look a little more closely to find unique shops and offerings in this Black Hills city.

ALEX JOHNSON MERCANTILE

(523 Sixth St. ☎ 605.343.2383) The Alex Johnson Mercantile is a small but unique gift shop, featuring sculptures, art, jewelry, and crafts by local and regional artists. It's located in the historic Hotel Alex Johnson.

RUSHMORE MALL

(Interstate 90 & Lacrosse St. ☎ 605.348.3378
⛁ rushmoremall.com) If you need a "mall fix" while in the
Hills, this is the largest one in the region. Rushmore Mall is a
110-store mall with the typical mall eateries, shops and department stores.

PRAIRIE EDGE GALLERY

(Sixth & Main St. ☎ 605.342.3086 ⛁ prairieedge.com) Housed
in a historic downtown 1800s building, the store has a collection of Native American jewelry, arts, crafts and culture, as well
as Old West items. Started in the 1980s, the owners say they
want to educate the public about the Northern Plains Indians
and preserve their heritage and culture. It's a place for native
artists and craftspeople to sell their wares, including beadwork,
quill work, and art by painters, photographers, potters and
silversmiths. In the back of the store is the **Sioux Trading
Post**, where crafts enthusiasts can find a mix of traditional
and contemporary American Indian craft supplies, books and
botanicals.

SIOUX POTTERY

(1441 E. St. Joseph ☎ 605.341.3657 ⛁ siouxpottery.com)
Visitors take a self-guided factory tour at Sioux Pottery, and
then visit the factory outlet retail store. Each piece of pottery
is handcrafted by Sioux artists who decorate the pieces with
designs and symbols important to their culture. Each child
gets a free pot to decorate as they sit with the Lakota artists.
Shoppers can buy items online too. The studio is a member of
Indian Arts & Crafts Association.

The second-largest city in South Dakota, Rapid City, was founded in 1876 by a group of disheartened prospectors who showed up in search of gold.

Custer

This town in the southern Black Hills is small but offers motels, restaurants, and shops for visitors traveling between Hot Springs to the south, **Custer State Park** to the east and Hill City, **Mount Rushmore** and points beyond to the north.

The few blocks of urban setting surrounded by the forest and hills got its start like many Black Hills towns. Custer's roots are in the masses of miners who came looking for their fortunes in the late 1800s.

Early settlers at first couldn't agree on a town name when it was formed in 1875. They were Civil War veterans, and those from the north—a little less than half—wanted to name the town Stonewall in honor of their war hero Stonewall Jackson. Confederate Army veterans, however, favored honoring General Custer, who at the time was making a name for himself.

When mining days waned, the town of nearly 10,000 decreased to 14 people, whose names still are noted in the city's official records. By the end of 1876 the population again grew, this time to about 123 people. Notice the city's wide streets, built to accommodate covered freight wagon drivers who needed to make U-turns with their teams. Today the population is around 1,800.

Fort Welikit Car & Camper Rentals *(675 W. Mt. Rushmore Rd., Custer* ☎ *605.673.6600* 🖱 *blackhillsrv.net)* has travel trailers, ATVs, mopeds, SUVs and minivan rentals. For general information about Custer, contact the **Custer Chamber of Commerce** *(615 Washington St.* ☎ *605.673.2244* 🖱 *custersd.com).*

ATTRACTIONS

The old **Flintstone's** tourist attraction and campground is within the Custer city limits, but many attractions are a few miles from the town proper, including **Jewel Cave National Monument**, the second-largest cave system in the world, about 13 miles to the west. Both helicopter and hot-air balloon ride businesses are based here too.

FLINTSTONE'S BEDROCK CITY THEME PARK & CAMPGROUND

(422 W. Mt. Rushmore Rd., US Hwys 16/385 ☎ 605.673.4079
⬤ flintstonesbedrockcity.com) This kids' theme park has a train ride, houses patterned after the classic animated TV series, and a little playground for the kids, too. The park has been around since 1965, when the television show still aired new episodes in prime time. Snacks are available, with silly names for hamburgers, hotdogs and chicken—like Brontoburgers and fries, Dino Dogs and Chickasaurus. There also are ice cream treats. This attraction may have seen better days, but it still draws visitors who enjoy the Flintstone's theme. Camping and cabins are available, or visitors can just check out the small theme park, May through September. ($)

BLACK HILLS BALLOONS

(West end of Mt. Rushmore Rd. ☎ 605.673.2520
⬤ blackhillsballoons.com) Located adjacent to the Flintstone's Village, the only time of day flights are available is sunrise, when winds are calm and cool. Balloons only launch when weather is clear. The flight is about an hour in the air, but a three-hour activity including the inflation and launch, ending pack-up, and champagne toast. It's an expensive glide over the

Black Hills at about $250 per person, less for kids. Balloons can hold from two to 12 people per ride. The company says that the federally regulated aircraft are periodically inspected, and pilots are federally licensed commercial balloon pilots. ($$$)

BLACK HILLS AERIAL ADVENTURES
(Between Hill City & Custer, 24564 Hwy 16/385

☎ **605.673.2163** 🖰 **coptertours.com)** Helicopter tours take visitors above a portion of the Black Hills. There are a couple of very short tours—a few minutes—for reasonable fees. There are five tours, including more expensive, longer flights that take a look at the **Crazy Horse Memorial** and **Mount Rushmore** from above. Check out extensive video footage on the company's website. Call for current pricing. ($$$)

NATIONAL MUSEUM OF WOODCARVING
(Hwy 16 West, just west of Custer ☎ **605.673.4404**

🖰 **blackhills.com/woodcarving)** There's a gallery of wood carvings here and a gift shop, but the most interesting attraction is when a carver is in the studio creating a new piece. There usually is an artist in house during the summer months, and the attraction brings in different teachers for class sessions throughout the summer. ($)

1881 CUSTER COUNTY COURTHOUSE MUSEUM
(411 Mt. Rushmore Rd. ☎ **605.673.2443**

🖰 **1881courthousemuseum.com)** History buffs may want to stop by just see the building itself, the original Dakota Territory courthouse built in 1880-1881. Listed on the National Register of Historic Places, it served as courthouse, meeting place for church services, socials, and community activities for nearly

100 years before it was given to the Custer County Historical Society in 1973. Today it houses information about General Custer's expeditions to the area in 1874, the gold rush era, and the decades that followed. It's a short stop, where admission is free, but donations are welcome.

FOUR MILE OLD WEST TOWN

(11921 West US. Hwy 16, 4 miles west of Custer ☎ 605.673.3905 🖥 fourmilesd.com) Walking self-guided tours are available anytime from opening in May until closing in October, and by appointment during the off season. Formerly the town of Moss City, people called it Four Mile since the earliest stagecoach lines came through the area. It's a rustic setting, but has many storefronts housing artifacts that are tagged to explain what they are and how they were used. The doors are open and visitors are invited to touch the artifacts. There's a Wild West reenactment Fridays from Memorial Day through Labor Day. Other living history demonstrations and skits also are presented. ($)

JEWEL CAVE NATIONAL MONUMENT ✪ Must See!

(Off Hwy 16, about 13 miles west of Custer, 11149 US Hwy 16 ☎ 605.673.8300 🖥 nps.gov/jeca) Before you get to the second-largest cave system in the world, decide how much underground hiking you want to do, or are able to do. Bring a coat or sweater—it's 49 degrees deep beneath the ground, year-round. There are several levels of guided exploration to choose from in the more than 150 miles of maze-like passages. In the decades after it was discovered in 1908, Jewel Cave was thought to only be about a mile long. But during the past 40 years, exploration has revealed an extensive network of passages that perhaps are yet not fully mapped. The minerals are not precious jewels that could be made into jewelry—the glittering calcite crystals and a variety of colorful and rare cave formations are too soft—but are beautiful on the cave walls.

The easiest visit is simply a ride down an elevator to a large cavern, a walk down a few wide, clean metal-grated steps to a large metal deck where visitors stand and listen to a guide who tells facts about the cave. The next level of exertion is moderately strenuous, but an easy walk exploring along a paved, lighted trail. It goes up and down 723 steps scattered along a half-mile route that takes about an hour and a half. It's a good hike for kids who are able to walk that far. Children of all ages are welcome on the tour, but two- and three-year-olds probably can't manage the whole route. Big purses and baby backpacks are not allowed in this cave, and rangers want you to have both hands free to hang onto rails, so carrying kids through the cave is discouraged.

Other longer, harder tours range from hikers using mountain climbing techniques, to wriggling on your belly through tight spaces. One tour is a re-creation of old days using lanterns on a rigorous guided tour deep into far reaches of the cave. On February 7, 1908, President Theodore Roosevelt signed a proclamation to protect the cave. In 2008, Jewel Cave National Monument celebrated its centennial with a series of events and programs to highlight the anniversary. ($)

DINING

There are a few chains along Custer's main drag, Mount Rushmore Road, including **Pizza Hut**, **Subway**, **Quiznos**, **Dairy**

Queen and **Taco John's**. **The Cattleman's Steakhouse** *(140 Mount Rushmore Rd. a 605.673.4402)* has a big gift shop, a realistic tipi from the movie set of *Dances with Wolves* (filmed in the area) and food that serves its purpose for families cruising through the area. Dig a little deeper, however, and you'll find a few gems.

SAGE CREEK GRILLE

(611 Mt. Rushmore Rd. ☎ 605.673.2424) The restaurant has a smallish menu but serves above-average food, with a premier wine and beer list. There's a comfortable, easy atmosphere here, with excellent service. Favorites: buffalo tenderloin and walleye. A must-try when available is the smoked buffalo brisket. Some folks also swear by the pasta side dishes. They have rustic breads, and it's one of the few places that serve South Dakota Certified Beef. Closed on Sundays. ($$)

DARK HORSE STEAK & BREW

(140 Mt. Rushmore Rd. ☎ 605.673.3833) The Cajun ribeye is a treat, the filet mignon has a good reputation, and the steaks are a decent size. Dinner prices may not be for the budget conscious. More reasonable are the big lunch burgers, and there are a couple of dozen cold beers on tap. The atmosphere is interesting: steel sculpture and hand-painted horses, many by area artists. ($$)

DAKOTA COWBOY INN RESTAURANT

(216 W. Mt. Rushmore Rd. ☎ 605.673.4613) When there are lots of local folks eating here, you know the place has to be doing well. This two-story, Alamo/Southwestern-style building has a huge parking lot, and inside a cowboy atmosphere. Visitors find reasonable prices for many cuts of meat. Service is great, and the food is consistently good. Their soups are hearty, food is served in generous portions, and the seasoning is done right.

The location may be a little noisy for folks thinking about staying at the hotel, but there is a heated pool and mini-golf course on the property. Ask about the polecat burger. ($$)

PURPLE PIE PLACE

(19 Mt. Rushmore Rd. ☎ 605.673.4070 🦷 purplepieplace.com) Serving hundreds of slices of pie a week, this colorful, cozy little storefront makes homemade pies. Must try: strawberry rhubarb pie with huckleberry ice cream. Or try one of the more than a dozen ice cream flavors. This is a well-kept place that appeals to all ages. ($)

HOTELS

Find some chains and privately owned places along Mount Rushmore Road, but there are other offerings near town, too, nestled back in the forest or on hilly grounds. Some have cabins on the property for an experience different from the usual strip motel rooms.

HOLIDAY INN EXPRESS

(433 W. Mt. Rushmore Rd. ☎ 605.673.2500) New in 2008, there is a man-made waterfall in the back of the hotel and a large patio with tables and chairs. A fire pit is lit nightly. Some large rooms have two TVs, and a balcony with a couple of chairs and table that overlook the waterfall. Other rooms overlook the Flintstone campground next door. This hotel features big, soft comforters, plush towels and granite bathroom counter-tops. There's a good variety at the complimentary breakfast, in a nice setting with a fireplace. ($$)

AMERICAN PRESIDENTS RESORT CABINS & CAMP
(1 mile east of Custer on Hwy 16A ☎ 605.673.3373 🖱 presidentsresort.com) This is a sister property of the All American Inn, with cabins ranging from small, to larger with kitchens. There are no dishes, cookware or utensils provided. Most of the little cabins are named for U.S. presidents and are surrounded by mature trees. Larger units are available that sleep from four to 12 people. There is a 60- by 40-foot heated swimming pool and spa on the grounds with a 5,000-square-foot deck, a volleyball court, free mini-golf, horseshoes and a giant playground for the kids. There are campsites too. ($$)

COMFORT INN AND SUITES
(301 Mt. Rushmore Rd. ☎ 605.673.3221 🖱 comfortinn.com) Three-story brick chain hotel, large rooms with generous counter space, and a light continental breakfast. ($$)

BAVARIAN INN MOTEL
(One mile North of Custer on Hwy 16/385 North ☎ 605.673.2802 🖱 bavarianinnsd.com) Natural setting, heated pools—one indoors with cozy wood-walls, the other a large outdoor pool. There's also tennis courts (the office supplies rackets and balls), a good restaurant on the grounds and a lounge. Most rooms have an outside balcony for a better look at the surroundings. ($/$$)

CALAMITY PEAK LODGE

(Two miles east of Custer on Hwy 16A ☎ 605.673.2357
🖱 blackhills.com/calamitypeak) This is an older but comfortable motel with one- and two-bedroom units, some with sofa beds and kitchens. There's also a two-bedroom lodge house with a dining room and a furnished kitchen. All rooms are nonsmoking. Rooms ($); lodge house ($$).

ROCK CREST LODGE AND CABINS

(15 W. Mount Rushmore Rd. ☎ 605.673.4323
🖱 rockcrestlodge.com) These are comfortable, clean, newer cabins on the hill, so there's a good view of the area. A motel-like line of rooms is easy access, but there are stairs to climb to get to the nearby cabins—some are on a steep grade. Breakfast provided by the lodge is minimal. You can bring cereal or breakfast items to eat in the cabin. Located on 10 acres that feature a picnic area with several outdoor grills and a playground. ($$)

WAY BACK INN

(26699 Remington Rd. ☎ 605.673.2742 🖱 waybackinn.net)
Located 22 miles from the nearest paved road, this new, rustic-wooden house can accommodate up to six people. It has two fireplaces, kitchen and dinettes, phone, two TVs, three bedrooms and a loft with two bunk beds. There is a full bathroom and a half bath. Taxidermy buffalo and deer heads stare at guests in the main hall. ($$)

BED & BREAKFASTS

Bed and Breakfasts in and around Custer can offer a more personal experience than the traditional hotels in the area.

CUSTER MANSION BED & BREAKFAST

(35 Centennial Dr. ☎ 605.673.3333 🖱 custermansionbb.com)
Hang out and talk to other guests in this five-guest-room, 100-year-old house with seven gables. Wireless Internet is provided, and there's an outdoor Jacuzzi spa. Home-cooked breakfast is offered every morning. Originally built by a sheep rancher and farmer, the building also has served as the county's retirement home, a preschool, a local church, mini-mall, a tourist attraction known as "Monster Mansion," and a rental home. In 1988 it was restored as one of the first bed and breakfasts in the southern Black Hills. Each room is named after a song and decorated accordingly. ($) ($$)

STRUTTON INN BED & BREAKFAST

**(12046 Hwy 16, 3 miles west of Custer ☎ 605.673.2395
🖱 bnblist.com/sd/strutton/)** This is a huge, nine-room country Victorian inn, with fresh coffee ready at 6:30 a.m. and breakfast in the formal dining room from 8:30 to 9 a.m. Complimentary evening snacks with coffee, cappuccino, hot chocolate or lemonade are served 4 to 7 p.m. There's a large cowboy/American Indian-style decorated den featuring a 46-inch TV. All bedrooms have a king-size bed with canopy draping, private bath with Jacuzzi tub (single or oversized), and all have air conditioning and ceiling fans. ($$)

CAMPING

Sleep in a tipi. Or maybe put the gang up in a rough-hewn log cabin that sleeps four to 14 people. Custer and the surrounding area have many campgrounds, next to lakes, set back in the pines, and combined with RV and trailer parks.

BEAVER LAKE CAMPGROUND
(12005 W. Hwy 16 ☎ 605.673.2464

☗ beaverlakecampground.net) Tent camping and RV sites are here, and also several sizes of cabins with air conditioning, heating, electricity, hardwood floors and knotty pine walls. Each site has a fire pit and picnic table. No bedding or towels are provided, but are available for a fee. There also are tipis with a raised wooden floor. Pool and waterslide are available.

BIG PINE CAMPGROUND
(12084 Big Pine Rd. ☎ 605.673.4054

☗ bigpinecampground.com) The site has two bathhouses with hot showers, large wooded campsites, wireless Internet, and a gift shop. There are 90 sites, 75 with water and electric, 40 with sewer.

CUSTER MOUNTAIN CABINS & CAMPGROUND
(12503 E. Hwy 16A ☎ 605.673.5440

☗ custermountain.com) Rough-hewn log cabins sleep four to 14 people. All kitchen utensils and linens are provided in the larger cabins. There are also RV sites with full hookups, and tent sites—some close to the shower and laundry facilities, while some are remote wilderness sites.

ECHO VALLEY PARK

(12129 Echo Valley Rd. ☎ 605.673.3368 🖰 echovalleypark.com)
The park is located three and a half miles north of Custer, next to Crazy Horse Mountain. Large shaded tent sites, RV sites and full hookup sites are available. There also is a camping cabin that sleeps five.

HERITAGE VILLAGE CAMPGROUND

(24855 Village Ave. ☎ 605.673.5005 🖰 heritage-village.com)
There are tent sites, sleeping cabins and tipis, as well as RV hookups. A bathhouse and laundry are on site, and there's a little grocery store and restaurant too. Guided horseback rides available.

Custer

Custer State Park

━━━ ★

(☎ 605.255.4515 🖱 custerstatepark.info) A few miles east of the town of Custer is the huge state park that bears the same name. There's a fee, but it is worth the cost to see a broad variety of wildlife and scenery in this 71,000-acre park at the southeast corner of the Black Hills. One of the few remaining wild places in the United States, Custer State Park is just south of the town of Keystone and north, adjacent to Wind Cave National Park land.

There are thousands of camping spots in the second-largest state park in America, and it is home to more than 1,000 buffalo and other wildlife. Look for the Peter Norbeck Visitor Center in the northeast part of the park, on U.S. Highway 16A. There you can find answers to questions about the many forms of recreation available in the park.

The mountain lakes here are perfect for kayaking, canoeing and paddle boating. There's also horseback riding, safari-style Jeep tours, panning for gold and fishing. Travelers who want to stay will find many rental lodges and scenic campgrounds. There are resorts at Sylvan Lake, Legion Lake, Blue Bell and at the State Game Lodge. Horseback adventures are available.

An annual buffalo roundup, an event held each fall, involves moving thousands of these huge, woolly creatures that pound their hoofs in a massive group run, shaking the earth. Read more about the roundup online and see a **video** (🖱 *travelsd.com*).

More than 1,500 buffalo roam the prairies and hills in this park. Other wildlife includes elk, bighorn sheep, wild turkey and mountain goats. Wild burros (donkeys) sometimes block the road and investigate car windows looking for food hand-outs (discouraged) at the south part of the park. Visitors often spot bald eagles, badgers and porcupines, as well as marmots, antelope, coyotes, and mule and white-tailed deer. It's a large geographic area, so it's not uncommon for bobcats to roam the region too. Watch out for rattlesnakes on your walks.

Drive with care, as the animals roam free. Besides burros, drivers sometimes find themselves stopped for a herd of buffalo on the roadway. A large portion of the Black Hills is called the Norbeck Wildlife Preserve, established in 1920 for the protection of game animals and birds, and recognized as a breeding place for wildlife. The preserve covers about 35,000 acres, most managed by the U.S. Forest Service—thousands of acres are located in the park.

There are four state park lodges in the park, so you'll see their names repeated in two sections as we outline details about lodging there, and later each for each lodge's food offerings unique to each location.

The wildlife and scenery are the stars here in Custer State Park, and campgrounds abound for those who like to be close to nature. Many day trips are available throughout the park. Take a cruise along the twists and turns of Needles Highway in the northwest corner of the park, or along the open range along Wildlife Loop Road in the southeast part of the park.

NEEDLES HIGHWAY ✪ Must See!

(South Dakota State Hwy 87/Northwest Custer State Park) The 14 miles of winding roadway is an excellent way to see unique features of the Black Hills from the car. The narrow roadway has several small tunnels through granite mountains along sharp twists and turns, and plenty of pull-offs for a better look at the landscape or for exploring. The name Needles refers to the thousands of slender granite formations and unique rock outcroppings weathered by centuries of erosion. Among all the needles, one particular spire is a landmark granite rock formation that looks like the eye of a needle. It's about 40 feet high, with the "eye" several feet across.

Travelers must pay the state park admission to enter the northwest corner of Custer State Park, just southeast of Sylvan Lake, so the trip could be combined with more Custer exploration. A few spots along the road are aligned for travelers to catch a glimpse of the famous faces of Mount Rushmore, one at the other end of a short tunnel. It's a fun drive through the scenery, and there are easy walks along several hiking trails throughout the area. Experienced climbers may opt for scaling the many spires. ($)

SYLVAN LAKE

(24572 Hwy 87 ☎ 605.574.2561 ☋ custerresorts.com) This area was considered the jewel of the Black Hills when the state park was created in 1921, and many still call it one of their favorite spots in the Hills. Hike around this beautiful lake, or get out on the glassy, still water with boat and water sport rentals. The paddleboats have a capacity of three to five people, and the rowboats have a capacity of four. Hydrobikes are there for rent too. Anyone under age 18 must be with an adult, and the staff requires that everyone wear a furnished life jacket.

Other nearby lakes include Legion Lake (which also has mountain bike rentals) just off U.S. Highway 16A at Needles

Highway; Center Lake just off County Road 753 near Black Hills Playhouse; and Stockade Lake, three miles east of Custer on U.S. Highway 16. Cold Brook and Cottonwood Reservoirs are just north and west of Hot Springs.

THE BLACK HILLS PLAYHOUSE

(County Rd. 753 just north off State Hwy 87 ☎ 605.255.4141 ☗ blackhillsplayhouse.com) Set in the middle of the forest in Custer State Park, this summer theater and training program has been staging shows since 1946. The venue was the subject of some controversy in 2010 during state budget sessions. For that year's summer season, the Playhouse took its company on the road with plays at three different locations in the Black Hills. Be sure to call for the current location status. It is associated with the College of Fine Arts at the University of South Dakota. Actors, directors and designers come from across the country. Some shows aren't suitable for children. A state park entry sticker is required to get into the grounds, tucked back in the forest in the northern part of the park. ($$)

WILDLIFE LOOP ROAD

An 18-mile road swings through the southern section of Custer State Park. It connects south State Highway 87 and with west State Highway 16A. A good way to get a look at the park is by automobile. Grazing buffalo sometimes wander onto the highway, forming a living roadblock, so keep a sharp eye out for these wild creatures. Rangers warn that buffalo can be dangerous, so never try to approach them.

WIND CAVE NATIONAL PARK ✪ Must See!

(South adjacent to Custer State Park; 11 miles north of Hot Springs on US Hwy 385 ☎ 605.745.4600 🖰 nps.gov/wica) This is an interesting and easy hike through one of the world's oldest caves, so far mapped at more than 127 miles of passages—it's the third-longest cave in the United States, fourth in the world.

There are few stalactites and stalagmites, but unusual formations and minerals are seen during a guided walk. The cave is known for its "boxwork" crisscross formations made of thin calcite fins that look like honeycombs. While not too strenuous, it is a little tricky in spots, so less fit or unsteady visitors probably should pass on the cave tour. Cave trails are dimly lit and surfaces are sometimes uneven, wet and slippery. Some of the cave ceilings are low, requiring bending or stooping.

The visitors center has hand-written journals starting in 1881 by brothers Jesse and Tom Bingham, explorers who kept detailed notes for decades telling what they found in the cave. The center has three exhibit rooms, and an 18-minute movie is shown throughout the day. The brothers found Wind Cave when they heard a loud whistling noise, which led them to a small hole in the ground. So far that spot is the cave's only known natural opening.

Above the cave system are nearly 30,000 acres of protected mixed-grass prairie, Ponderosa pine forest and wildlife. Here visitors will spot some of the 400-450 buffalo, and also elk, pronghorn, mule deer, coyotes and prairie dogs. It's one of the last natural, undisturbed expanses of prairie grasses left in the nation. There are three self-guided nature trails and eight backcountry trails in the park. Information sheets and maps are

Custer State Paek

available at the visitors center information desk. Hiking cross-country is permitted. ($)

DINING

The four main eating establishments in this region also are the four best places to spend the night: Sylvan Lake, Blue Bell, Legion Lake and the State Game Lodge. As for the food, each offers very different menus, prices and eating experiences. They offer hearty ranch-style breakfasts, pack box lunches for hikes and outings, prepare wild game from the region, and offer fine dining.

SYLVAN LAKE LODGE RESTAURANT

(24572 Hwy 87 ☎ 605.574.2561 🖱 custerresorts.com) The buffalo steaks are a specialty, but remember that they're a lot leaner than beef. That makes them seem tougher and dryer, depending on how they're prepared. But health experts say that's good for a healthy diet. The Sylvan Lake chefs make a great fresh-water trout for fish lovers, and the Wapiti (Elk) tenderloin. There's a breakfast buffet and lunches, and for a fee the lodge will pack travelers a box lunch for picnics. The dining room and terrace have a great view of the lake and Harney Peak. Breakfast/Lunch ($) Dinner ($$$)

BLUE BELL LODGE RESTAURANT

(25453 Hwy 87 ☎ 605.255.4531 🖱 custerresorts.com) This location offers dining in a rustic log cabin-like eating area. On the menu is buffalo steak and fresh trout, but also items not often found elsewhere like the Blue Bell's classic buffalo meatloaf or the potato-encrusted salmon. The "Fireside Buffalo

Skillet Tips" are a nice change from the usual. They're mari-
nated and griddled together with onions and mushrooms in a
cast-iron skillet, served with vegetable and fries. Breakfasts and
lunches are offered, and a chuck wagon cookout is available.
($$)

LEGION LAKE LODGE RESTAURANT

(13389 US Hwy 16A ☎ 605.255.4521 🖰 custerresorts.com) Less
formal than the other lodges in the area, there's a deli, bakery
and burger joint at this lodge, casual dining for breakfasts,
lunch and dinner. Hot and cold sandwiches, burgers, and hot
dogs are among the offerings. Fresh-baked pies include apple,
cherry, blueberry, peach or pumpkin. Many sizes of pizza are
here too. ($)

STATE GAME LODGE RESTAURANT

(13389 US Hwy 16A ☎ 605.255.4772 🖰 custerresorts.com)
Buffalo, pheasant and other wild games are the specialty of
this lodge restaurant. The eatery has been featured on TV's
Food Network. Dishes include grilled elk chops, buffalo filet
mignon and venison tenderloin. There's a lodge lunch buffet
that includes fresh fruits and vegetables and the chef's hot-bar
selections, and breakfasts are also available. The Custer State
Park buffalo stew is a must-try. ($$)

LODGING

Visitors will find the gracious stone and wood architecture of
Sylvan Lake Lodge and the **State Game Lodge** in the state
park, or the more modest wood construction of **Legion Lake**
and **Blue Bell** lodges. All are nestled amidst the towering Pon-

derosa pines, with lots of room to roam on the surrounding grounds.

SYLVAN LAKE LODGE

(24572 Hwy 87 ☎ 605.574.2561 ⬤ custerresorts.com) This is one of the most attractive areas of the Black Hills, with a classic view of the historic lake, forest and rock formations. After the original lakeshore resort burned down in 1935, architect Frank Lloyd Wright suggested the current location in the forest of pine and spruce trees. It's got an old-style big lodge feel, built with lots of natural stone and wood, starting with the lobby's wide wood-plank floors and tall, beamed ceiling. There's also a lounge and restaurant. Lodge-style rooms are a classy mixture of historic and modern. Several cabins are available nearby, scattered among the pine and spruce forest. The one-room cabins have fireplaces and TVs. Housekeeping cabins are larger. ($$)

BLUE BELL LODGE

(25453 SD Hwy 87 ☎ 605.255.4531 ⬤ custerresorts.com) Every cabin has a fire pit outside. Nestled in full-grown pines, there are small sleeping cabins, and larger four person and six-person cabins. Heavy, round-beamed ceilings and rustic decor fit in nicely with the location. Also offered here are horseback riding and a chuck wagon-style dinner. ($$)

LEGION LAKE LODGE

(13389 US Hwy 16A ☎ 605.255.4521 ⬤ custerresorts.com) Built directly on the water's edge, there are paddleboat, rowboat and hydrobike rentals on this lake, which is named for the American Legion Post that once leased the land. There are a variety of small to family-size cabins here, with and without kitchens or kitchenettes. There's an on-site store offering deli, bakery goods and burgers at this casual lakeside setting. ($$)

STATE GAME LODGE

(13389 US Hwy 16A ☎ 605.255.4541 🖱 custerresorts.com) A newer section called Creekside Lodge opened in 2008 with 30 luxurious, oversized lodge rooms, a big lobby and great room, and two meeting rooms. In the older historic lodge there also are rooms, and on the grounds are motel units and cabins with and without kitchens or kitchenettes. Activities at the lodge include the Buffalo Safari Jeep Tour, a Jeep ride, the Chuck Wagon Cookout Adventure. ($$)

There are thousands of camping spots in Custer State Park, which is the second largest state park in America.

Hot Springs

The last sizable town at the south end of the Black Hills is quaint, quiet and picturesque. Hike along the Freedom Trail that winds its way along the banks of the Fall River. There are a few shops, galleries, coffee houses, bookstores, restaurants and lounges in the century-old sandstone buildings found here.

Check out the 1890 railroad depot that now serves as a Visitor Information Center in the historic Sandstone District on North River Street.

The town site was originally was called *minnekahta*, or "warm waters" by European settlers in the late 1800s, but the name soon was changed to Hot Springs. Earlier, the Lakota and the Cheyenne Native American tribes fought for control of the natural warm springs. Legends tell of a hostile encounter fought in the hills above the springs on a peak called Battle Mountain.

By 1890, residents, including a businessman named Fred Evans, tried to take advantage of the warm mineral waters and capitalize on the medicinal properties some say they have. He built the original Evans Plunge business over a group of small springs and one large thermal spout of warm mineral water. It still exists today as an indoor swimming pool attraction.

For general information about Hot Springs, contact the **Hot Springs Chamber of Commerce** *(801 S. Sixth St.* ☎ *605.745.4140* 🖱 *hotsprings-sd.com)*.

Hot Springs

ATTRACTIONS

There are a few places to dip into indoor waters from the region, living up to the town's name. But Hot Springs also is recognized as having the best Ice Age fossils in the world, at the Mammoth Site. From the mini-golf course to the museum, there are a few offerings for visitors.

THE MAMMOTH SITE ✪ Must See!

(US Hwy 18 bypass at Hot Springs ☎ 605.745.6017 ☋ mammothsite.com) Very few of the ancient woolly mammoth bones found here have been moved from their original resting places, making the Mammoth Site the best Ice Age fossils on earth, presented in a permanent display. It's the world's largest Columbian mammoth exhibit, a world-renowned research center for Pleistocene studies. Visitors can see the laboratory in the basement and watch scientists working with fossils.

Videos and diagrams tell how unfortunate woolly mammoths came to drink from a sinkhole 26,000 years ago and often fell in. The sides were too steep and slippery to get back out. So far, 55 well-preserved skeletons are left in place with the ancient soil excavated away at this indoor excavation site, leaving an interesting bed of dozens of mammoths for visitors to see all year. There's also an Ice Age exhibit hall featuring a full-sized mammoth replica, a walk-in mammoth bone shelter and an extensive book selection for sale in the gift shop. ($)

EVANS PLUNGE

(1145 N. River St. ☎ 605.745.5165 ☋ evansplunge.com) Because the human body is at about 98.6°F, the town's namesake waters don't feel hot at 87°F. And there are no natural surroundings for swimming here at Evans Plunge, as the town's name may suggest. Instead, this attraction is a commercial building, an indoor swimming pool filled from spring-fed sources. Billed as the world's largest naturally heated indoor swimming pool, the entire pool of water turns over with fresh mineral water every hour and a half. That's 16 times in a 24-hour period. There are some waterpark-like attractions here, including water slides and some Tarzan Rings to swing out over the water. Upstairs is a workout room. ($)

PIONEER HISTORICAL MUSEUM

(300 N. River St. ☎ 650.745.5147 📱 pioneer-museum.com) This four-story sandstone building was built in 1893 and used as a school until 1961. It's located on the hill between upper and lower Hot Springs. Today it houses handcrafted tools of farmers and ranchers, including washing machines, wood cook stoves and kerosene lamps. There's also a display of an old doctor's office, a 19th century classroom and county store. ($)

PUTT-4-FUN HOT SPRINGS MINI GOLF

(640 S. 6th St. ☎ 605.745.7888 📱 putt4fun.us) Landscaped with native rocks, this 18-hole mini-golf course has two water fountains, a few sand traps and a waterfall. It's next to the Host Hills Inn. ($)

SPRINGS BATH HOUSE

(146 North Garden St. ☎ 605.745.4424) Water and massage therapies are offered at Springs Bath House that features one outdoor and three indoor pools of different temperatures. Kids can come, but the staff suggests that they visit the Evans Plunge waterpark nearby, or take the supervised Mammoth Site tour while parents are pampered by what some say are healing properties of the natural mineral waters. ($/$$)

BLACK HILLS WILD HORSE SANCTUARY
(14 miles south of Hot Springs off Hwy 71 ☎ 605.745.5955 ☗ wildmustangs.com) Tours are available here only by reservation. There's a two-hour guided bus tour, a three-hour cross-country tour, and a six-hour "adventure" tour. Visitors board a bus and are driven out into the heart of this 11,000-acre region where wild horses truly run free through prairies, canyons, hills and rivers. The driver keeps a lookout for groups of horses, and pulls up close so that visitors can get a closer look or photograph the American Spanish, Sulphur and Kiger Mustangs. Some animals are from herds from state governments, the Bureau of Land Management and the U.S. Forest Service.

The sanctuary is not just a tourist attraction, but a nonprofit refuge started by cowboy Dayton O. Hyde in the 1980s when he saw America's surviving wild mustangs being rounded up and sent to slaughter. Tours include a look at Native American ceremonial sites and ancient rock drawings called petroglyphs. There's also a special four-hour guided tour available especially for photographers. For extra fees, spend two or more nights in a modern but rustic log cabin overlooking the Cheyenne River, year-round. It sleeps four, has air conditioning and cable TV, but no phone or Internet service. ($$)

DINING

Hot Springs offers the usual fast food-type offerings for folks in a hurry. There are casual stops, like the old-fashioned ice cream counter at the **Blue Bison** *(509 N. River St.* ☎ *605.745.3057)*, **Dale's Family Restaurant** *(745 Battle Mountain Ave.* ☎ *605.745.3028)*, **Woolly's Mammoth Family Fun** *(1403 Hwy 18 bypass next to Holiday Inn Express* ☎ *605.745.6414)* which includes a drive-up coffee kiosk, the **All Star Grill & Pub** *(310 S. Chicago St.* ☎ *605.745.7827)*, and **China Buffet** *(333 N. River St.* ☎ *605.745.4126)*. Take a little more time with other eateries:

THE BLUE VERVAIN

(At Red Rock River Resort & Spa/603 N. River St.
☎ **605.745.4400** 🖱 **bluevervain.com)** This restaurant gets top reviews but only serves an evening meal, and only on Tuesday through Saturday. French-Italian cuisine has a few touches of Asian and Southwest, too. The menu goes well beyond the usual steak and potatoes, on a par with top restaurants in large cities. Executive Chef Rebecca Christensen displays magazine articles for award-winning dishes at her previous location in Colorado.

The restaurant also employs a pastry chef who makes fine desserts and pastries. Sometimes there is a piano player on a grand piano in the restaurant/lounge area. Beverage bar includes coffee, espresso, old-fashioned ice cream sodas, and hot-fudge sundaes. There's lots of tea here, too, with a variety of black, green, white, rooibos and herbal blends. ($$/$$$)

BRAUN HOTEL & SPRING STEAK HOUSE

(902 N. River St. ☎ 605.745.3187 🖱 braunresort.com) Steaks are their specialty, and they do it pretty well. A ribeye and a filet mignon, both medium rare, were cooked properly on a recent trip. The salad bar has more than the usual fare, baked and mashed potatoes were flavorful, and an order of fresh vegetables is a healthy touch. But, annoying to some, each drink refill is an extra charge, even coffee. Patio dining available where visitors often can see deer wander up and graze in the yard. ($$)

FLATIRON COFFEE BAR & GRILL

(745 N. River Dr. ☎ 605.745.5301 🖱 flatiron.bz) Flatiron has homemade soups, good atmosphere, but not fast service. Try the white chicken chili when it's available, or a big piece of quiche and a cup of coffee. Orders are taken at the counter then brought to tables. It's an interesting location: the building is called the Gibson House, but it is actually known on the National Historic Register as the FlatIron Building. Open May through October. ($)

HOTELS

There's the usual budget fare, but also some unique places to stay in and near Hot Springs, like the Shangrila hunting lodge on the banks of the Cheyenne River, to interesting renovated downtown hotels in century old sandstone buildings. Red Rock has an easy-access spa in the historic building for some guest pampering.

RED ROCK RIVER RESORT & SPA

(603 N. River St. ☎ 605.745.4400 🖱 redrockriverresort.com)

Located in the downtown historic district, Red Rock is in a grand sandstone building constructed in 1891. Big rooms let you spread out with high ceilings and deep windowsills. Some nice touches are above-average bedding with down comforters and feather/down pillows. Along with the historic feel are modern conveniences, including air conditioning, private bath, and cable television. The restaurant is on the first floor, and rooms on the second and third floors. Very clean rooms, some with refrigerators and spacious showers.

There's no breakfast, but the beverage bar has coffees and teas. Accommodation packages include use of an excellent spa that offers a dry sauna, hot tub, hot sand room, hot granite floor room quiet area and massages in adjoining rooms. Great place to wind down after a day of sightseeing. ($/$$)

BEST WESTERN SUNDOWNER INN

(737 S. Sixth St. ☎ 605.745.7378 🖱 bestwestern.com)

Renovated in 2005, this 51-room hotel has an indoor swimming pool and hot tub, and guest laundry. Small pets, under 50 pounds only, are welcome. The executive suite has a two-person hot tub and a large-screen television. There is no elevator to the second floor. ($$)

BUDGET HOST HILLS INN

(640 S. Sixth St. ☎ 605.745.3130 🖱 budgethosthillsinn.com)

Outdoor pool is in the middle of the wide parking lot. There are 35 smallish but clean rooms, with double, queen, and king beds, refrigerators and microwaves. In true motel fashion,

Hot Springs

parking is at the door to the room. HBO and Disney Channel are included on the extended cable television offerings, and wireless high-speed Internet is available. ($)

FLATIRON GUEST SUITES

(745 N. River St. ☎ 605.745.5301 🖥 flatiron.bz) Furnished like cozy apartments, four suites are in the upper level of this historic building. The back patio is spacious and comfortable, with a grassy landscaped area and tables with umbrellas—a comfortable place to relax. The building is called the Gibson House, but it is actually known on the National Historic Register as the Flatiron Building, named after the first skyscraper in New York City that looks like an old-fashioned flat iron. ($$)

BISON RIVERSIDE INN

(646 S. Fifth St. ☎ 605.745.5191) Bison Riverside Inn features a cabin-like look, with wood ceilings. This hotel is close to the road, good for easy access, but a little noisy. A continental breakfast is offered, served from 6:30 to 8:30 a.m. ($$)

RODEWAY INN AT BATTLE MOUNTAIN

(402 Battle Mountain Ave. ☎ 605.745.3182) Rodeway Inn is an older, single-level motel with queen-size beds, refrigerator and microwave in the room. It's also known as the Dollar Inn. Continental breakfast is in a small area with coffee, mini muffins, orange juice and coffee cake. ($$)

SHANGRILA RANCH

(27743 Irrigation Road, near Oral and Hot Springs ☎ 605.343.2226 or 605.390.5280) This full-service hunting lodge, a 2,000-acre hunting preserve, is located on the banks of the Cheyenne River. The land is home to an abundance of wild game, including pheasants, ducks, geese, wild turkey and deer. Fish in the ponds, shoot sporting clays, spend an evening playing billiards or Texas hold 'em in the bar and game room. Packages for several nights are about $1,600 to $3,600, but include three meals a day with wine, guide dogs, field transportation, hunting licenses, bird cleaning, transportation to and from the airports, and more.

BED & BREAKFASTS

Two bed and breakfasts stand out in this area; both of them offer historic significance.

A DAKOTA DREAM BED & BREAKFAST

(801 Almond St. ☎ 605.745.4633) This 1891 bed and breakfast has an amazing view from the top of the hill, looking down onto the city of Hot Springs. It's the former 1891 Sioux City Gentleman's Gaming Club, and the third level still is set up with period pieces and poker table, as if time stood still. The building was renovated in 1990 as a six-bedroom bed and breakfast. Each room has a queen-size bed and private bath. They plan fun packages for guests including a honeymoon or anniversary, wedding and Murder Mystery Weekend. ($$$)

HISTORIC MUELLER HOUSE BED & BREAKFAST

(201 S. Sixth St. ☎ 605.745.5272

☻ muellerhousebedandbreakfast.com) Built by John Mueller, one of the founding residents of Hot Springs, this unassuming house offers satellite television in both parlor and cottage, and a fireplace in the parlor. The Victorian Room has a private bath, the Cottage and the Mueller Room share a bath, and the Cowboy Room and the Dakota Room also share a bath. ($/$$)

CAMPING

One of the area campgrounds features antique tractors, farming implements and acres of wildflowers. Another is located on a huge lake with four camping areas, a few miles south of town. The clear waters of Angostura Reservoir draw visitors, with plenty of room for boating, fishing and swimming off the natural sand beaches.

KEMO SABAY CAMPGROUND
(27288 Wind Cave Rd. ☎ 605.745.4397
🖰 kemosabaycampground.com) Located on 90 acres at the foot of Battle Mountain, this campground has a collection of antique tractors and farming implements. There are more than 40 kinds of wildflowers blooming at various times of the year near this quiet park, with 25 RV sites, acres of tent sites, bathrooms, showers and laundry. There's a new-looking cabin for rent here too.

ANGOSTURA RESERVOIR RECREATION AREA
(13157 N. Angostura Rd./South Dakota Division of Parks and Recreation ☎ 605.745.6996 🖰 southdakota.com) Located 10 miles southeast of Hot Springs off U.S. Highway 385/18, this big lake is great for boating, fishing and swimming. It has clear waters and natural sand beaches. The Bureau of Reclamation built the dam in 1949 across the Cheyenne River for irrigation purposes. There are four campgrounds, with Cascade (in the

north unit) and Horsehead (in the south unit), the largest of the four. Cheyenne (in the north unit) and Hat Creek (in the south unit) are the smaller ones. There are eight cabins here, too, overlooking the lake.

Besides camping and cabins, the area is great for all kinds of recreational activities. Besides biking and boating, there are three picnic shelters and an accessible hiking trail. You'll find a nine-hole disc golf course, and a game and equipment checkout service, a playground, horseshoe courts, a volleyball court, and canoe and kayak rentals.

*Much of the Badlands is "use" park,
meaning that you can explore almost
anywhere you like.*

Outside the Black Hills

South Dakota is a land of seemingly endless intrigue. Not far from the Black Hills, visitors may find themselves in a rocky, barren landscape, or near one of the world's most famous man-made roadside attractions.

All of southwestern South Dakota cannot be explored in one trip, or even 10 trips. Some attractions are great distances from each other, so any trips out of the Black Hills will need to be planned in advance—so try to avoid packing too much into one vacation. Accounting for travel time is necessary, as these are long roads.

BADLANDS NATIONAL PARK ★ Must See!

(South of Wall ☎ 605.433.5361 ● nps.gov/badl) The Badlands National Park region is a vast, otherworldly landscape more than 50 miles east of Rapid City and the Black Hills on Interstate 90. A fun way to take a look at the area by vehicle is to make the scenic 30-mile drive on State Highway 240, starting from either end of the loop road between the Interstate 90 Exit 110 or 131. The road follows the natural contours of a cliff-like ridge of land, and twists through the native grasslands. Scenic overlooks with names like Seabed Jungle, Pinnacles and Prairie Wind, offer great photo and hiking opportunities. There are lots of places to pull over and see sections of the landscape along the highway also known as Badlands Loop Road, a two-lane, paved surface.

Much of the Badlands is "use" park, meaning that you can explore almost anywhere you like. If you see a knife's edge cliff you want to scale off in the distance, you can give it a try. But most first-time visitors should stick close to the trails so they don't get lost. The entire park is open to you to explore by foot. There is no backcountry permit system and you are not limited to trails. However, all vehicles, including bicycles, must remain on designated roads.

A typical visit lasts three to five hours if you take in the 20-minute park movie shown throughout the day, stop at four overlooks, and walk on a couple of trails for a close-up look at the landscapes, native plants and wildlife on the mixed-grass prairie ecosystem. Many areas are a painted desert of jagged cliffs and odd ridges that go on for miles, giving the park a moon-like quality.

The region was created after millions of years of wear by wind and rain cutting out spires and canyons in this stark, barren land. The 244,000 acres of eroded buttes, pinnacles, and spires is open all year. Native Americans called the area *mako sika*, which in Lakota means "land bad," and early French trappers also described the area as "bad land" when they had trouble traveling over the rugged terrain.

There are five hiking trails, varying from a quarter mile to eight miles in length, and paths for horseback riders. There are several ranger-led programs in the summer months. In the South Unit, the **White River Visitors Center** is open during the summer. The remainder of the park is open to exploration, but you need to know what you're doing to avoid getting lost. Rangers recommend using a topographic map and a compass. The park service advises that only extreme adventurers should wander through the backcountry of the badlands.

The climate is variable and unpredictable, with temperatures ranging from 40 degrees below zero in the winter to well over 100 degrees during summer months. The weather can change quickly during a single day, and it's often a very windy place.

Camping is by permit only and not recommended for the inexperienced. The jagged landscape and buttes provide moderate to difficult hikes along miles of designated trails. Experienced hikers say that sturdy hiking shoes are needed to avoid injury.

Scientists working for the National Park Service say this area is the world's richest fossil beds, dating from about 30 million years ago. Learn more about the formations at the park's main **Ben Reifel Visitor Center** on the Loop Road. It's open daily all year except holidays. When the region was a spring-fed watering hole it attracted many animals. Paleontologists uncovered the remains of ancient three-toed horses, tiny deer-like creatures, turtles, a saber-toothed cat, dinosaur bones and other prehistoric animals that lived here.

Today the Badlands has vast areas of surrounding grasslands. Buffalo, bighorn sheep, endangered black-footed ferrets, and swift fox roam one of the largest, protected mixed-grass prairies in the United States. More than 64,000 acres of the park are designated as wilderness, home to hundred of prairie dogs that carve their towns throughout the plains of the park. There also are jackrabbits and cottontail rabbits sometimes seen running fast across the grassland where pronghorns graze. Mule deer, coyotes and badgers live in the canyons.

Half of Badlands National Park—the South Unit—is in the Pine Ridge Indian Reservation and contains several sites that are considered sacred to the Oglala Lakota. The National Park

Service and the tribe work together to co-manage and protect that part of the park, south of State Highway 44. It is mostly undeveloped and has only minimal access by road. ($)

WALL

Located about 56 miles east of Rapid City, millions of tourists stop in this small town just north of the Badlands each year, most to visit the famous **Wall Drug** store founded in 1931. Today the town has 12 motels to accommodate visitors coming and going to the Black Hills.

A series of formations nearby gave the town of Wall its name. The "wall" is a rugged strip of tinted spires, ridges and twisted gullies that ranges from a half mile to three miles wide and is over nine miles long. It stands between the great upper prairie flats and gentle grassy hills, according to the **Wall Badlands Area Chamber of Commerce** (☎ *605.279.2665* ⭗ *wall-badlands. com*).

Wall Drug is the best-known attraction, but what visitors might overlook are other attractions here, including the **National Grasslands Visitor Center**, where there's information about all 20 U.S. National Grasslands, the **Wounded Knee Museum**, a nearby **Minuteman Missile Site**, an **Old West 1880 Town**, and a prairie homestead.

WALL DRUG ✪ Must See!

(510 Main St. ☎ 605.279.2175 ⭗ walldrug.com) An hour east of the Black Hills, longtime tourist attraction, Wall Drug, is located on this small town's Main Street. Allow more than an hour to explore this rambling 76,000-square-foot complex. It has dozens of indoor retail storefronts, including collections of books, original handcrafted items, highly polished and raw colorful rocks and crystals, jewelry, fudge, and candy made on site, and souvenirs including kids' toys.

The five-cent cup of coffee and homemade cake donuts are visitor favorites. There's a large restaurant here, too, with dining areas that also serve as a Western art gallery of sorts—the owners display more than $1 million in original artwork by famous artists including American favorites Harvey Dunn, N.C. Wyeth, Will James and many more. Diners look at the paintings while eating from the large breakfast menu, and lunch and dinner items including buffalo ribeye steak, buffalo burgers, fish, and a garden burger made with an all-natural, meatless patty.

Both kids and adult visitors find a broad range of inexpensive souvenirs, some "Native American" items made overseas. But walk deeper into the complex and you'll find the real thing: handcrafted Native American and other styles of hand-made jewelry, boots and leather goods, and artwork. Kids can explore the Back Yard, with newer attractions like the "gold mine" that takes them into a dark, deep cavern to find shiny metallic rocks. There's a pan-for-gold kids' area, too.

On a hot day visitors may want to get in the way of small bursts of water that leap from hole to hole in a large outdoor patio. Nearby is a life-size, snarling animated T-Rex head that pops out from behind a high iron gate like a scene from *Jurassic Park*. Original attractions remain that generations of visitors saw as youngsters, like the rustic, animated life-size singing cowboys from the 1950s.

This sprawling, eclectic, mostly indoor attraction still is owned by the third generation of the Hustead family, who started it as a tiny drug store in 1931. Its rise to fame came when the Ted and Dorothy Hustead rightly guessed that travelers headed to the Black Hills and beyond during scorching hot summers would be thirsty. They put up a signs near the highway luring travelers in with the promise of free ice water, still offered today.

Road signs for this tourist stop have become a tradition in South Dakota and neighboring states, dotting the landscape for miles in a radius around Wall Drug. The signs also have become a game of sorts for fans of the attraction. They photograph the signs around the world telling the number of miles to Wall Drug from the ends of the earth, from Australia and China to the North and South Poles.

NATIONAL GRASSLANDS VISITOR CENTER

(708 Main St. ☎ 605.279.2125 ☗ fs.fed.us/grasslands) Located on Main Street in Wall, the center is headquarters is the National Grasslands Visitor Center, a one-stop place to learn about all 20 U.S. National Grasslands and the characteristics of each of them. South Dakota is home to the Buffalo Gap, Fort Pierre and Grand River National Grasslands. Located two blocks south of Wall Drug, the visitors center has an exhibit room and theater presentation. Buffalo Gap National Grasslands is nearby, just off Interstate 90 and surrounding Badlands National Park. It's more than a half-million acres, the second-largest grasslands in the country. One of the last undisturbed American frontiers, hikers can travel for many miles and never see a road or telephone pole.

WOUNDED KNEE: THE MUSEUM

(207 10th Ave, Wall ☎ 605.279.2573

⬤ woundedkneemuseum.org) This Wall museum tells the story of Lakota families who became the focus of the last major military operation of the U.S. Army. Exhibits and photographs tell about the events surrounding the massacre. It's carefully researched and well documented as a narrative museum devoted to the story of the Wounded Knee Massacre of 1890. Includes a gift shop, bookstore and trading post. Open May through October. ($)

MINUTEMAN MISSILE NATIONAL HISTORIC SITE

(S. side of Exit 131 off Interstate 90 ☎ 605.433.5552

⬤ nps.gov/mimi) A few miles west of Wall, this National Park Service site is 75 miles east of Rapid City, and just north of the eastern edge of the Badlands. It used to be one of many top secret Minuteman missile sites across the country that housed rockets armed with nuclear bombs that had the power to destroy large portions of the earth in faraway countries. The sites were decommissioned in the 1990s—there are no nukes here anymore. Due to limited space and high demand, reservations are strongly recommended. Tour reservations are taken up to one week in advance.

This site probably is of interest mostly to visitors who want to see first-hand an actual control center set up in the 1960s. There are exhibits and a park orientation video, which places the Minuteman missile program into historic context. The tour includes living areas, the concrete missile launch bay, and the control room where two key-holding men across the room from each other could have launched the warhead.

It's one of the newest National Park attractions in the nation, and still is working to expand its offerings. When rangers aren't there, a 10-stop, self-guided tour is available with recorded messages visitors can listen to on their cell phones.

PRAIRIE HOMESTEAD

(Exit 131 off Interstate 90, 21141 State Hwy 240 ☎ 605.515.0138 ☗ prairiehomestead.com) See what life was like for early settlers at this site, the original sod house of Mr. and Mrs. Ed Brown, who homesteaded the 160 acres in 1909. There has been some maintenance and minor restoration, but the buildings are virtually the same as they were back in the "sodbuster" era. The attraction claims it has the only white prairie dog town in the world, after more than 30 years of careful breeding of naturally occurring white prairie dogs. ($)

BADLANDS PETRIFIED GARDENS

(Interstate 90, at Exit 152, near Kadoka ☎ 605.837.2448 ☗ badlandspetrifiedgardens.com) This longtime family-owned attraction is of interest to both rock hounds and those interested in prehistoric fossils and petrified trees. It's also a good place to get a polished chunk of ancient petrified tree for a desktop conversation piece. Most large examples are in a homespun, outdoor backyard area, moved onto the grounds from throughout the Badlands and Black Hills region. One of the largest known examples of a fallen, petrified tree is here, estimated at more than 60 million years old. There are also sea life fossils scientists say could be more than 200 million years old, fossilized remains of a sabertooth tiger, bear dog, titanothere and other extinct animals. There is an extensive rock and gift shop, and a large display of regional minerals, agates, crystals and fluorescent minerals. Open April 15 through October 31. ($)

SOUTH DAKOTA'S ORIGINAL 1880 TOWN
(Interstate 90, Exit 170, near Murdo ☎ 605.344.2236
☊ 1880town.com) Get the feel of what it might have been like walking along the main drag in an Old West town. An inexpensive costume rental services lets visitors stroll the town in period clothing—good for picture-taking. Built in the early 1970s as a set for a movie that never was made, there are about 30 buildings, authentically furnished with relics from the time period. Included are some props used during the filming of a movie that did see the light of day: *Dances with Wolves*. Costume rentals are available for all ages and sizes in the Longhorn Saloon. Visitors can get in character, walk through the town, and take pictures. Hang around in the saloon and drink a cold sarsaparilla while listening to the player piano. ($)

PIONEER AUTO SHOW
(Interstate 90 & State Hwy 83, Murdo ☎ 605.669.2691
☊ pioneerautoshow.com) About 133 miles east of Rapid City (80 miles east of Wall) is a museum filled with about 275 cars from many decades. The 1969 orange Charger called the General Lee, used in the TV series *the Dukes of Hazzard*, is here. There are also 60 motorcycles—one of Elvis Presley's motorcycles is featured, tractors, music boxes, toys and rocks, as well as a re-created prairie village. There's also a large gift shop and a '50s-style diner. It's a long way from the Black Hills, but if you're traveling that direction on the way or leaving, it's a fun stop for vintage car enthusiasts. ($)

NORTHWEST OF THE BLACK HILLS

Driving northwest out of the Black Hills along Interstate 90 will eventually get you to Wyoming. Along the way, there are a few stops worthy of note.

DEVIL'S TOWER NATIONAL MONUMENT ✪ Must See!

(☎ 307.777.7777 ✆ wyomingtourism.org) The monument is about 60 miles northwest of Spearfish, in Wyoming. From Interstate 90 take either exit 154 (Moorcroft, Wyo .) or 185 (Sundance, Wyo ., then travel on U.S. Highway 14 north to State Highway 24 north. From the northwestern corner of the Black Hills of South Dakota, it's about 60 miles from Spearfish, S.D. , across the state line to this Wyoming landmark. Scientists call this natural rock formation a geologic wonder. It's a single, tree stump-shaped granite formation 1,267 feet high, like a stone skyscraper in the middle of the countryside.

There is a bit of a climb between the parking lot and the trail around Devil's Tower, but it's a level, easy walk. Give yourself over an hour to walk around the base, or just walk a section of the path. Visitors see many different views up the rock columns, and at the landscape below. Geologists say the formation was in the ground, but over thousands of years of erosion the weather stripped away dirt and softer rock, leaving the rock tower. It was a major location for the movie *Close Encounters of the Third Kind*.

Take time to check out the adjacent fields of prairie dogs—fun creatures to watch, but signs warn that feeding can harm them. Open year-round, and around the clock, the Devil's Tower visitors center is open from early April to the end of November.

There's lots of information there, or at the administration building during winter months.

During the summer, rangers give talks about the natural and cultural history of the area. There's a trail that's about a mile and a half long that circles the base of the monument and takes hikers along the rubble of thousands of years that have fallen from the tower—huge columns of rock. There's also a longer three-mile trail for hikers who want more of a challenge.

There are campgrounds here, too, and picnic areas. Evening ranger-led programs are in the amphitheater. The site is sacred to Native Americans, who tell a legend about how a giant bear clawed the grooves into the mountainside while chasing young maidens. Mountain climbers need a permit to scale the rock face to the top, which is about 275 feet across at the top compared to about 1,000 feet at the bottom.

There is lots of wildlife, so watch for birds, chipmunks, snakes and more. Exhibits at the visitors center and park programs help visitors understand the area. It's also a great place for bicycle riding and photography. There is gas, food and hotels in the nearby towns of Hulett, Sundance and Moorcroft. ($$)

BELLE FOURCHE

(Chamber of Commerce, 415 Fifth Ave. ☎ 605.892.2676
⛶ bellefourche.org) This small town is the geographical center of the United States, designated in 1959 and noted by an official marker and sheepherder's monument called a "Stone Johnnie." Businesses and antique shops have located in the early 1900-era buildings downtown, the western part of the

state's largest reservoir is a more than 8,000-surface-acre lake, fishing area and campground. It's also home to the more than 80-year-old Black Hills Roundup Rodeo. The rodeo, held around July 4 each year, also features a parade, carnival and fireworks.

The town name is French for "beautiful fork," named by French explorers who stopped here at what is now where the Belle Fourche and Redwater rivers and Hay Creek meet. Beaver trappers worked here until the mid-1800s, when Belle Fourche was a well-known fur-trading area.

In 1895 a fire destroyed most of the downtown business district, but it was rebuilt, partially with structures moved in from nearby Minnesela. Many of these buildings remain today. On June 27, 1897, Kid Curry of the Hole-in-the-Wall Gang (along with Butch Cassidy and the Sundance Kid), botched the robbery of the Butte County Bank here, now a modern bank.

Today the town still serves a large trade area of ranches and farms. The wool, cattle and bentonite industries have been important to the growth of the town. **The Center of the Nation Wool Company** is here *(820 8th Ave.* ☎ *605.892.6311)*, owned by sheep producers, warehouses thousands of bales that are sent around the world. It doesn't process the raw wool, but instead markets the wool to buyers. It's an impressive warehouse, packed floor to ceiling with huge bales of wool. The staff is friendly to wool spinners who want to take a look, although small batches are not for sale here.

TRI-STATE MUSEUM

(415 Fifth Ave. Belle Fourche ☎ 605.723.1200 ☗ thetristatemuseum.com) This free museum has exhibits of early pioneer days, rodeos and Old West history. The original 1876 Johnny Spalding Cabin is here, along with artifacts from the early days of raising cattle in the region. The Belle Fourche Visitor Information Center is in the same complex as the Tri-State Museum. Outside decks lead to a large, attractive Geographic Center of the Nation monument. Nice place for visitors to take pictures at the center of the nation.

ROCKY POINT RECREATION AREA

(8 miles east of Belle Fourche off State Hwy 212, 18593 Fisherman's Road ☎ 605.584.3896) The Belle Fourche Reservoir is the largest reservoir lake in western South Dakota, at more than 8,000-surface-acres of water. The Rocky Point park is a new South Dakota State Park. It opened in 2006 with dozens of electrical campsites, five group camping pods, showers and flush toilets, a dump station, boat ramps and fish cleaning station , paved roads, picnic shelters and play equipment. Kayak rentals and boat ramps are available. ($)

The extensive Centennial Trail links Custer State Park, Bear Butte State Park and Wind Cave National Park.

Outdoor Activities

The Black Hills is a dream come true for those drawn to the Great Outdoors. During your vacation, even the most indoor-hardy people will feel a pull to join in the outdoor fun.

HIKING AND BIKING

Mountain bikers get their knobby tires onto hundreds of miles of old logging trails and un-maintained roads throughout the Black Hills, as well as along trails developed for riding. Hikers can trek off onto forest trails most anywhere. Those who need more structure will find many marked and groomed paths that make it a little easier to hoof it through the hills.

The larger cities have nicely maintained urban bicycle paths, including Rapid City, Spearfish and Sturgis. Many of the lodges have mountain bike and hiking trails leading from their grounds into the National Forest, usually well-marked paths. In areas where serious hikers take longer trips, there is long-term parking provided at the trailheads. Notify rangers in the state and national parks if you plan to park for several days, and leave messages with someone about the trails you will be hiking or biking. Wherever you end up, make sure everything you bring into the park comes back out. Carry your own drinking water because there is none available along the trails. Open fires are allowed only in designated picnic areas and campgrounds—there have been several forest fire disasters during the past few decades.

At the southeastern corner of the Black Hills, Custer State Park's 71,000 acres alone offer nearly endless days of hiking. There's the Sylvan Lake shore trails, a creekside trail between the State

Game Lodge and Coolidge General Store, and about 20 other designated trails. Maps are available at park ranger stations.

Besides designated trails, hiking is allowed nearly anywhere in the parks. The extensive Centennial Trail links Custer State Park, Bear Butte State Park and Wind Cave National Park. Most established trails are marked by blue diamonds fastened to trees. The Centennial Trail is marked by gray diamonds and brown fiberglass posts.

Along the way, don't feed wildlife, watch out for rattlesnakes sometimes seen in the parks. There's a warning from rangers at Custer State Park of mountain lions living in the Black Hills, so if hikers find themselves face to face, they shouldn't run. Park officials say that you must maintain eye contact with the lion, talk and yell at it, gather children close and make yourself appear as large as possible. Become aggressive by throwing objects or waving sticks.

SOUTH DAKOTA CENTENNIAL TRAIL

(☎ 605.225.4464 ☗ southdakota.com/centennial-trail/107) This 111-mile trail spans the length of the Black Hills, climbing south from the plains near Bear Butte State Park in the north, winding through rugged, heavily forested interior lands, to the prairies at Wind Cave National Park in the South. It is the longest continuous recreational trail in the Great Plains region.

About 22 miles are in Custer State Park. The trail was opened in June 1989 to commemorate the South Dakota centennial. Horse riders sometimes use the trail too. Several government land management agencies develope and supervise different portions of the trial, so there are different rules for different sections. Each has their own variations on regulations, so check the section you plan to visit. For example, mountain bikes are not allowed in the Black Elk Wilderness. In other areas, ATVs and horses share the trail. Hiking is allowed along the entire length.

THE GEORGE S. MICKELSON TRAIL

(☎ 605.584.3896 ⬤ sdgfp.info/Parks) From its northern-most end through Lead and Deadwood, to the southern end of the Black Hills at Edgemont, the more than 100-mile-long Mickelson Trail accommodates hikers and bicyclists who are looking for a way to explore the Black Hills. Named after the late former South Dakota governor, the trail is converted from no-longer-used railroad beds, including more than 100 train bridges and four hard rock tunnels. Completed in September 1998, it's designed for people of all ages and abilities.

Most of the trail is in National Forests, but there are portions that pass through privately owned lan—that's where people must stay on the trail. Each September for more than a decade, hundreds of bicycle riders join the Annual Mickelson Trail Trek, a 109-mile, three-day ride. The event began in 1998 as a celebration of the completion of the rails-to-trails project. The event continues as a way to introduce new bicyclists to the pathway and to thank supporters for their long-standing enthusiasm for the trail. There are both daily and annual passes to use the trail. ($/$$).

HARNEY PEAK

(Near Sylvan Lake) You don't have to be a mountain climber to hike to the top of Harney Peak, the highest point in South Dakota. But you do have to be in somewhat decent shape.

A round-trip hike from Sylvan Lake can take more than four hours. An impressive granite, treeless peak at 7,242 feet, it's the highest point in the United States east of the Rocky Mountains.

Experienced hikers suggest wearing tough hiking boots, and to bring along a light jacket even in the summer. It's an amazing view from the top—you can see into surrounding states, and there's a cool old fire-lookout station at the very top that is no longer in use, but is open to hikers.

There are a few routes to the peak; the shortest is a three-mile path starting in Custer State Park (park fee required) at Sylvan Lake, Trail No. 9. The trail is marked with blue diamonds. A little longer trail is Trail No. 4. The most difficult trail leads up from Highway 244 near Horse Thief Lake. It's a U.S. Forest Service-maintained trail. Get maps from the Custer State Park entrance kiosks or at any U.S. Forest Service office. No paid permits are necessary, but registration is required because the peak is in the Black Elk Wilderness. There's a self-service kiosk where you register and receive a permit on the way to the summit.

GRACE COOLIDGE WALK-IN FISHING AREA

This is an easy walk or bicycle ride along Grace Coolidge Creek, about 10 miles east of Custer. Get to it off State Highway 87 to County Road 359 (Black Hills Playhouse Rd.) and then northeast to the Center Lake access road. The south end of the trail is just across the road from the Grace Coolidge Campgrounds (on U.S. Highway 16A, about a quarter mile west of the park headquarters). This is a three-mile, one-way trail. Fishermen will find lots of trout in this stream.

FRENCH CREEK NATURAL AREA

(Custer State Park) French Creek is a small stream that runs east-west through Custer State Park. George Custer made the little river famous during the summer of 1874 when prospectors from the Custer Expedition discovered gold. The specks of gold found in French Creek caused a fury of gold seekers who rushed into the Black Hills. The French Creek Natural Area is a 12-mile backcountry hiking trail. It was established to protect the natural resources at French Creek Gorge.

BLACK HILLS HIKING GROUP

(🖰 blackhillshiking.multiply.com) This nonprofit group of hiking enthusiasts provides comprehensive online information including organization of maps, trail descriptions, photos, and Internet links for hiking and backpacking in the Black Hills and Badlands region. Related trail activities such as snowshoeing, cross-country skiing and cycling are also included, and there's a section devoted to wheelchair-accessible trails. Check out their blog to see what other hikers have been up to in the Hills.

BLACK HILLS ADVENTURE TOURS

(Rapid City ☎ 605.209.7817 🖰 blackhillsadventuretours.com) For folks not comfortable heading out to hike on their own, Carrie Bowers, a longtime resident of the Black Hills, offers a variety of family-friendly adventure tours as well as specialty tours. Beginners and the more extreme outdoor enthusiasts who like to hike, bicycle and kayak will get help finding and navigating the region. Her company is permitted by the National Forest Service to guide visitors on Mickelson Trail bike rides, Badlands, Black Hills and Spearfish Canyon hikes, and kayak outings on Sylvan, Deerfield and Pactola lakes.

SYLVAN ROCKS

(Hill City ☎ 605.484.7585 🖰 sylvanrocks.com) This climbing instruction and guide company has been at it since 1989. Adventures range from mild to difficult climbs in the Black Hills. No previous experience is needed. Favorite areas are Custer State Park and Mount Rushmore. Accredited by the American Mountain Guides Association.

HORSEBACK RIDING

Riding horses is an up-close and personal way to see the Black Hills, but beginners may get sore. Novices should take an hour ride before attempting longer rides, perhaps the next day, to see how they feel. There's often a 250-pound per rider limit, so call ahead to see if heavier people may ride. At some stables the horses are well trained, so be sure to tell the office your real riding experience level, and don't exaggerate. Riders who know horses well usually get an animal that needs more direction than a beginner's horse.

On hot summer days, the morning ride is the best option to beat the heat of the day. Streamline the check-in process and reserve your time by stopping by the stable the day before to fill out paperwork.

PARADISE VALLEY TRAIL RIDES

(Boxelder Forks Road, Nemo ☎ 605.578.1249 🖰 paradisevalleyadventures.com) Several different types of rides are available for all levels of experience. Large groups are welcome, but reservations are encouraged.

GUNSEL HORSE ADVENTURES

(Near Rapid City ☎ 605.343.7608

⬤ gunselhorseadventures.com/BlackHills) Four-day trips include trail riding through canyons and rivers, with a look at lots of wildlife including deer and buffalo herds. Participants also listen to poems and cowboy songs each evening around the campfire.

HIGH COUNTRY GUEST RANCH

(12172 Deerfield Road, Hill City ☎ 307.266.9003

⬤ highcountryranch.com) This is a Western-style guest ranch in a secluded wilderness setting, but with modern comforts. Horseback riders must be age six or older—pony rides are available for younger kids. There are no trail rides on Sundays.

RECREATIONAL ADVENTURES CO.

(12620 State Hwy 244, Hill City ☎ 605.574.3412) Camping and lodging is found at Palmer Gulch at the Mount Rushmore/Hill City KOA and resort. Palmer Gulch Stables offers daily horseback trips. Cowboy breakfast and dinner rides are available.

HOLY SMOKE TRAIL RIDES

(US Hwy 16A south of Keystone ☎ 605.666.4616

⬤ blackhills.com/holysmoke) You get a couple of good looks at Mount Rushmore on this ride, which is the closest trail ride to the monument. One- and two-hour rides are available throughout the Black Hills National Forest.

HERITAGE VILLAGE CAMPGROUND

(24855 Village Ave., Custer ☎ 605.673.5005

⬤ heritage-village.com) This attraction is located one mile south of Crazy Horse Memorial on U.S. Highway 16/385, or four miles north of the town of Custer. It specializes in small groups for a variety of guided rides ranging from one-hour, one-and-a-half, and two-hour rides. There's a half-day options for riders of all ages and experience levels. An overnight ride is also available.

BLUE BELL STABLES AND TRAIL RIDES

(Blue Bell Lodge, 25453 SD Hwy 87, Custer ☎ 605.255.4700
☗ **custerresorts.com/blue-bell-lodge)** This stable offers one-hour, two-hour, half-day and full-day rides. Children under age four can't ride, and children over age four must ride alone. Call a day ahead to sign up for the breakfast trail ride. The short trails are good for first-time and novice riders, families with children and beginners who would like a sightseeing nature ride. All-day rides are for experienced riders, comfortable in the saddle for hours at a time, who want to explore the backwoods of Custer State Park.

COUNTRY CHARM CABINS & CORRALS

(11863 West Argyle Rd., Custer ☎ 605.673.2686
☗ **countrycharmcabins-corrals.com)** There are guided trail rides for visitors to this campground. Also on site are cabin rentals and a horse corral for people who bring their own horses. The staff is good at matching various horses with riders of all ages and abilities.

BADLANDS RANCH AND RESORT

(Interior, S of Badlands ☎ 605.433.5599
☗ **badlandsranchandresort.com)** Badlands Ranch offers a ride through the Badlands. An hour-and-a-half ride takes visitors

through varied terrain, for all ages and riding skills. This location also has camping and RV spaces, motel rooms, and a bed and breakfast.

PALMER GULCH STABLES

(Dakota Badlands Outfitters, 12620 Hwy 244 ☎ 605.574.3412 🖱 ridesouthdakota.com) From horseback rides to equipment for people with horses and stable pens, there are many options available through this group for horseback riding throughout the Black Hills. Riders select from several options, including the Norbeck Wildlife Preserve, a cowboy breakfast ride, the Black Elk Wilderness and a chuck wagon dinner ride. The stables are located at the KOA campground five 5 miles west of Mount Rushmore. ($/$$/$$$)

HORSE CAMPS

Many people bring their own horses with them to ride in the Black Hills. They can ride on their own or join weekend treks organized by local horse clubs. There are horse camps throughout the Black Hills, some primitive, but others with lots of extras like staff, corrals, water wells, feed bunks and picket posts.

WILLOW CREEK HORSE CAMP

(7 miles southeast of Hill City ☎ 650.574.4402) Reservations are required in the summer; four days in advance is recommended. Camping is free in the winter. There are restrooms on site. Directions: Take U.S. Highway 16/385 from Hill City, and travel south seven miles; then travel east on State Highway 244. The campground is across from the Mount Rushmore KOA.

ELK HAVEN HORSE CAMP AND RESORT

(Hwy 16-A, 24654 Iron Mountain Rd, Keystone
☎ **605.666.4856** 🚻 **elkhavenhorsecamp.com)** This horse camp is near Keystone, with a lodge on site. It's a quaint building with a covered porch running full length across the front. There are campsites, covered corrals for the horses, extra corral panels, fire pits, campsite grills and picnic tables. There's a grocery store on site too. Horse trails match various degrees of riding skill. Easy rides include lush meadows or rides around the lakes, while longer trails head deeper into the Black Hills and along some rough, challenging trails. Take a full day—eight or nine hours round trip—to get to the Mouth Rushmore area. Trails also head south to Custer State Park.

IRON CREEK HORSE CAMP

(12 miles northeast of Custer ☎ **605.574.4402)** This campground is adjacent to Iron Creek, renovated in 1996. There are corrals and restrooms here. Get there by traveling east on U.S. Highway 16A from Custer, about eight miles to State Highway 87, then north for about four miles on Forest Service Road 345 for about a mile to the access road.

FRENCH CREEK RANCH BED & BREAKFAST

(25042 Kemp Dr., Custer ☎ **605.673.4790**
🚻 **frenchcreekranch.com)** This is a modern ranch-style lodge that boasts about not having any Victorian lace and ruffles. It's a horse ranch, decorated with Western and Native American artwork. There also a sauna, a game room with pool table, large fireplace, wet bar with refrigerator, private guest patio with outdoor wood-burning chimney, and a picnic table and gas barbecue grill. Sports fans will find tennis, basketball and

volleyball courts. There are fishing opportunities nearby too.
($/$$)

SPIRIT HORSE ESCAPE
(11596 W. Hwy 16, Custer ☎ 605.673.6005

☗ **spirithorseescape.com)** Guests choose cabins with kitchens, bathrooms, and one to three bedroom. Porches overlook the forest. Larger groups can rent cabins for up to 10 adults. For those with horses there is a washhouse with full baths. Surrounded by Black Hills National Forest land, there are many miles of good riding trails. Those who stay may want to try the large four-person tipis on wooden platforms. Bring your own bedroll. ($)

DEERFIELD LAKE RESORT
(11321 Gillette Prairie Rd. ☎ 605.574.2636

☗ **deerfieldlakeresort.com)** Tent camping, RV electric or full hookups and cabins are here on this lake west of Hill City, on Forest Service Road 17. Laundry and shower facilities are on site. No dogs are allowed. Snowmobilers, ATV riders and both fishing and hunting guests also stay here. Extra fees are charged for use of the standard corral or the newer enclosed barn. Water is close to most pens. ($/$$)

GOLF

There are many golf courses from which to choose in and around the Black Hills area. Even if you're not a professional golfer, you can still have a fun day golfing. It is recommended that you call in advance to book your golf outing.

SPEARFISH CANYON COUNTRY CLUB

(120 Spearfish Canyon Dr./US Hwy 14A and Colorado Boulevard, Spearfish ☎ 605.717.4653 🖰 spearfishcanyoncountryclub.com) This is an 18-hole championship golf course in the northern Black Hills. On the grounds are an outdoor heated swimming pool, bar and grill, golf shop and practice range. A golf professional is on staff at the semi-private club near the entrance to Spearfish Canyon.

FOUNTAIN SPRINGS GOLF CLUB

(1750 Fountain Plaza Dr., Rapid City ☎ 605.342.4653 🖰 fountainspringsgolf.com) On Interstate 90, just off the Deadwood Avenue exit. The course has nine holes with a variety of water features, trees and landscapes. Patio and barbecue facilities are available. With water on every hole, watch for turtles, geese, birds and other wildlife along the course. Weather permitting, the course is open year-round. This course is part of the Fountain Springs community of homes, townhouses, senior apartments and a children's center.

RAPID CITY ELKS GOLF COURSE

(3333 E 39th St., Rapid City ☎ 605.393.0522) The front nine winds through creekside grounds where golfers often see wildlife sharing a fairway. Wetland preserves on the back nine are nesting grounds for many birds. Elevated tees make for a great view.

EXECUTIVE GOLF COURSE

(200 12th St., Rapid City, off Omaha St. at Interstate 90, Exit 57 ☎ 605.394.4124) Walkers like this landscaped nine-hole course with two par-fours and seven par-threes. Located along Rapid Creek, club rentals and a snack bar are available.

GOLF CLUB AT RED ROCK

(6520 Birkdale Dr., Rapid City ☎ 605.718.4710

🖱 golfclubatredrock.com) This 18-hole course offers dramatic elevation changes, rolling fairways and an outstanding practice facility. Including target greens, short-game practice area, and a large updated practice green. Native fescue grasses and tall Ponderosa pines surround the course. Lunch and dinner are served at the Red Rock Bar & Grill.

MEADOWBROOK GOLF COURSE

(3625 Jackson Blvd., Rapid City ☎ 605.394.4191

🖱 golfatmeadowbrook.com) Rapid Creek flows through the course and comes into play on five of the 18 holes. Meadowbrook was named one of the "Top 50" public courses in the nation in 1990. There are PGA professionals and assistants available for lessons by appointment. Host of the 2009-2010 NAIA Women's National Golf Championship, players will find a golf shop, rentals, driving range and coffee shop.

LA CROIX GOLF COURSE

(3820 Odde Dr., South Rapid City ☎ 605.718.9953) This nine-hole course on the YMCA golf grounds is an easy walk for child, adult and senior golfers. It's a good course for beginners and novices. Both the clubhouse and the golf course are available for family events, company meetings, picnics or events.

HART RANCH GOLF COURSE

(23645 Clubhouse Dr. ☎ 605.341.5703 🖱 hartranch.com) Hart
Ranch is located about 10 minutes south of Rapid City. There
is a beginner-friendly short course within the regular 18-hole
course, so players of all ages and ability levels can play Hart
Ranch. It has been listed in listed in *Golf Digest*'s "Places to
Play." Surrounded by Ponderosa pines, it has a full-service golf
shop, practice course, cart and club rentals and a snack bar.

ROCKY KNOLLS GOLF

(West side of the City of Custer on Hwy 16 ☎ 605.673.4481)
Rock outcroppings are found in the area of this nine-hole
layout. The course starts with a difficult par five, with play
through some of the unique rock formations. This short layout
has three sets of tee boxes.

SOUTHERN HILLS MUNICIPAL GOLF COURSE

(West of Hot Springs along US Hwy 18 ☎ 605.745.6400
🖱 **hotsprings-sd.com)** Ranked as the No. 1 nine-hole course in
North America in 1999 by *Golf Digest*, this municipal course
has since been expanded to an 18-hole course. It also was
chosen as one of the finest 36 courses in the Midwest. Playing
through is like a nature walk, with lots of wildlife and natural
surroundings. The course is amid pine-covered hills, meadows,
ravines and rock outcroppings.

Index

1880 Town 187
1880 Train 103
1881 Custer County Courthouse Museum 147

Adams Museum 69
airports 25
Alex Johnson Mercantile 142
Alkali Ike Tours 68
Alpine Inn 106
Alpine Inn Lodging 109
American Presidents Resort Cabins & Camp 152
Anchorage Bed & Breakfast 127
Angostura Reservoir Recreation Area 176
Antique Emporium 73
automobile, getting around by 26

Badger Clark Hometown Cowboy Music and Poetry Gathering 42
Badlands Petrified Gardens 186
Badlands Ranch and Resort 200
Barefoot Resort 65
Bavarian Inn Motel 152
Bay Leaf Cafe 48
Bear Butte State Park 86
Bear Country U.S.A. 93
Beautiful Rushmore Cave 122
Beaver Lake Campground 155
Belle Fourche 189
Best Western Black Hills Lodge 51
Best Western Four Presidents Lodge 125
Best Western Sundowner Inn 173
Big Pine Campground 155
Big Thunder Gold Mine 119
Bison Riverside Inn 174
Black Hills Adventure Tours 197
Black Hills Aerial Adventures 147
Black Hills Balloons 146
Black Hills Bluegrass Festival 37
Black Hills Caverns 95
Black Hills Community Theater 137

Black Hills Corvette Classic 39
Black Hills Fat Tire Mountain Bike Festival 35
Black Hills Ft. Pierre Railroad Roundhouse Restaurant 62
Black Hills Glass Blowers 121
Black Hills Gold 21
Black Hills Hideaway Bed & Breakfast 81
Black Hills Hiking Group 197
Black Hills Maze Family Adventure Park 133
Black Hills Mining Museum 58
Black Hills Overdrive All-Car Rally 36
Black Hills Playhouse, The 160
Black Hills Powwow & Arts Expo 42
Black Hills Quilter's Guild Show 38
Black Hills Roundup Rodeo, The 39
Black Hills Wild Horse Sanctuary 170
Blue Bell Lodge 164
Blue Bell Lodge Restaurant 162
Blue Bell Stables and Trail Rides 200
Blue Vervain, The 171
Boondocks 78
Boot Hill Tours 68
Borglum Historical Center 121
Braun Hotel & Spring Steak House 172
Broken Boot Gold Mine 69
Budget Host Hills Inn 173
Buffalo Rock Lodge 128
Buffalo Roundup 41
Bumpin' Buffalo Bar & Grill 106
bus lines 26

Cadillac Jack's 75
Calamity Peak Lodge 153
Car Rally & Demo Derby 38
car rentals 131
Carvers Café 122

Cedar House Restaurant 50
Celebrity Hotel 80
Central States Fair and Rodeo 40
Chapel in the Hills 136
Cheyenne Crossing Store and B&B 63
Cheyenne Crossing Store and B&B 64
Chubby Chipmunk Hand-Dipped Chocolates 73
Circle B Chuckwagon 124
City of Presidents 134
Cleghorn Springs State Fish Hatchery 135
Colonial House Restaurant 140
Colorful Past 19
Comfort Inn 107
Comfort Inn and Suites 152
Comfort Inn Gulches of Fun 79
Corn Exchange 138
Cosmos Mystery Area 93
Country Charm Cabins & Corrals 200
Country Manor Bed and Breakfast 110
Coyote Blues Village Bed & Breakfast 111
Crazy Horse Memorial 91
Crazy Horse Memorial Day Weekend 35
Crazy Horse Stampede / Gift From Mother Earth Celebration 36
Crazy Horse Volksmarch 36
Crooked Creek Resorts Campground 112
Crystal Cave Park 95
Custer Mansion Bed & Breakfast 154
Custer Mountain Cabins & Campground 155

Dahl Fine Arts Center 135
Dakota Cowboy Inn Restaurant 150
Dakota Dream Bed & Breakfast, A 175
Dakota Quilt Company 55
Dark Horse Steak & Brew 150
Days End RV Park 89

Days of '76 Museum 71
Days of '76 Museum & Camp 82
Days of '76 Rodeo 38
D.C. Booth Historic National Fish Hatchery 45
Deadwood Gulch Resort & Gaming 76, 79
Deadwood Jam 41
Deadwood Thymes Cafe & Bistro 78
Deer Mountain 61
Deerfield Lake Reservoir 99
Deerfield Lake Resort 100, 112, 203
Deerview Bed & Breakfast 111
Delmonico Grill 139
Desperados Cowboy Restaurant 107
Devil's Tower National Monument 188
Dinosaur Park 136

Eagles' View Air Tours 46
Echo Valley Park 156
Econo Lodge of Mt. Rushmore Memorial 125
Elk Haven Horse Camp and Resort 202
Elkhorn Ridge RV Resort & Cabins 54
Elk Ridge Bed & Breakfast 128
Emerald Pines Bed & Breakfast 111
Evans Plunge 168
Executive Golf Course 204
Executive Order Grill 124

Fairfield Inn & Suites 141
Festival in the Park Art Show 39
Firehouse Brewing Company 138
Fireworks 38
Fish 'n Fry Campground 82
Flags and Wheels Indoor Racing 136
Flatiron Coffee Bar & Grill 172
Flatiron Guest Suites 174
Flintstone's Bedrock City Theme Park & Campground 146
Flying T Chuckwagon Supper and Show 140
Focus West Gallery 55

Fort Hays Chuckwagon Supper and Show 96
Fountain Springs Golf Club 204
Four Mile Old West Town 148
French Creek Natural Area 197
French Creek Ranch Bed & Breakfast 202

Gathering of the Clans Dakota Celtic Festival 41
George S. Mickelson Trail 195
Gold Discovery Days 40
Golden Corral 140
Golden Hills Resorts & Convention Centers 64
Golden Phoenix 140
Golden Spike Inn and Suites 109
gold mining 20
Golf Club at Red Rock 205
Grace Coolidge Walk-In Fishing Area 196
Gradinaru's Haus of Kaffee 63
Green Bean Coffeehouse 50
Guadalajara Mexican Restaurant 50
Gunsel Horse Adventures 199

Harney Peak 195
Hart Ranch Golf Course 206
Heritage Village Campground 156
Heritage Village Campground 199
High Country Guest Ranch 199
High Plains Western Heritage Center 45
Historic Adams House 70
Historic Homestake Opera House 59
Historic Mueller House Bed & Breakfast 175
Holiday Inn Express 88, 126, 151
Holly House Bed & Breakfast 111
Holy Smoke Trail Rides 199
Holy Terror Days 42
Homestake Mine 58
Horse Thief Campground and RV Resort 113
Horsethief Lake 100
hospitals 33
Hotel Alex Johnson 141

Iron Creek Horse Camp 202

Jewel Cave National Monument 148
Jon Crane Gallery 102
Journey Museum 134

K Bar S Lodge 126
K Bar S Lodge Restaurant 123
Kemo Sabay Campground 176
Kemp's Kamp 129
Kevin Costner's Original Deadwood Tours 68
Keystone Historical Museum 121

La Croix Golf Course 205
Legends B&B and Log Cabin Suites 89
Legion Lake Lodge 164
Legion Lake Lodge Restaurant 163
Lewie's Saloon & Eatery 61
Lode Stone Motel and Cabins 107
Lodge at Deadwood, The 75
Lucky's 13 Pub 50

Mammoth Site, The 168
maps, 32
Meadowbrook Golf Course 205
Memorial Park and Berlin Wall Exhibit 137
Mickelson Trail Bicycle Trek 41
Midnight Star 74
Mineral Palace Hotel and Gaming 80
Minuteman Missile National Historic Site 185
Mistletoe Ranch 105
Motorcycle Museum and Hall of Fame 88
Mountains to Prairie B&B 110
Mountain View Campground 54
Mountain View Lodge 108
Mount Moriah Cemetery 70
Mount Rushmore July 3-4 Celebration 39
Mount Rushmore National Memorial 116
Museum of Geology 134
Museum of Natural History 102

Mystic Hills Campground 83
Mystic Miner Ski Resort 61

National Grasslands Visitor Center 184
National Museum of Woodcarving 147
National Presidential Wax Museum 120
Needles Highway 158
newspapers 33
Newton Fork Ranch 109

Old MacDonald's Petting Farm 96
online information 32

Packing for Your Trip 31
Pactola Pines Marina 97
Pactola Reservoir 97
Palmer Gulch Stables 201
Paradise Valley Trail Rides 198
Peggy's Place 125
Peregrine Pointe Bed & Breakfast 142
Petrified Forest of the Black Hills 90
Pioneer Auto Show 187
Pioneer Historical Museum 169
Powder House Lodge 126
Powder House Steakhouse 123
Prairie Berry Winery 104
Prairie Edge Gallery 143
Prairie Homestead 186
President's Park 59
Purple Pie Place 151
Putt-4-Fun Hot Springs Mini Golf 169
Putz n Glo 96

Rafter J-Bar Ranch 113
Ranch Amusement Park, The 96
Rapid City Elks Golf Course 204
Recreational Adventures Co. 199
Recreational Springs Resort 65
Red Rock River Resort & Spa 173
Reptile Gardens 92
Rock Crest Lodge and Cabins 153
Rocky Knolls Golf 206
Rocky Point Recreation Area 191
Rodeway Inn at Battle Mountain 174

Roma's Ristorante 49
Roubaix Lake 83
Ruby House Restaurant 123
Rushmore Express 127
Rushmore Mall 143
Rushmore Waterslide Park 133

Sage Creek Grille 150
Saigon Restaurant 139
Saloon No. 10 / Deadwood Social Club 76
Sand Creek Bed & Breakfast 53
Sanford's Grub & Pub 47
Seasons and Temperatures 29
Secret Garden Bed & Breakfast 53
Shangrila Ranch 174
Sheridan Lake 98
Sheridan Lake Marina 98
Shoot The Bull Steakhouse 48
sightseeing bus tours 27
Silverado Franklin 76
Sioux Pottery 143
Sitting Bull Crystal Caverns 95
South Dakota Air and Space Museum, The 137
South Dakota Centennial Trail 194
Southern Hills Municipal Golf Course 206
Spearfish Canyon Country Club 204
Spearfish Canyon Lodge 48, 52
Spearfish Canyon Scenic Byway 44
Spearfish Chophouse and Whiskey Bar 49
Spearfish City Campground 54
Spirit Horse Escape 203
Spirit of the Hills Wildlife Sanctuary 47
Spokane Creek Cabins and Campground 129
Spring Creek Inn 108
Springs Bath House 169
Stampmill Inn and Restaurant 62
State Game Lodge 165
State Game Lodge Restaurant 163
Storybook Island 133
Strawberry Bed & Breakfast 81
Strutton Inn Bed & Breakfast 154

Index

Sturgis Cavalry Days Celebration,
    Art Show 37
Sturgis Motorcycle Rally 40, 87
Sturgis Mustang Rally 88
Sylvan Lake 159
Sylvan Lake Lodge 164
Sylvan Lake Lodge Restaurant 162
Sylvan Rocks 198

Tally's 139
Tatanka: Story of the Bison 71
taxi services 131
Termesphere Gallery 46
Terry Peak Ski Area 60
Thunderhead Underground Falls 94
Timber Lodge Retreats and RV Park
    114
Tramway: President's Alpine Slide
    and Rushmore Tramway 119

Travelodge of Spearfish 51
Trial of Jack McCall 71
Tri-State Museum 191
Trout Haven 72

Wade's Gold Mill Mining Museum
    105
Wall Drug 182
Way Back Inn 153
Whistler Gulch Campground 82
Wild Bill Days 35
Wildlife Loop Road 160
Willow Creek Horse Camp 201
Wind Cave National Park 161
Wonderland Cave 90
Wounded Knee: The Museum 185

Yesterday's Inn Bed and Breakfast
    52

About the Author

Jay Kirschenmann is both a full-time news and feature writer for a national news service and a musician. He's based in Sioux Falls, South Dakota, where he writes about local and national artists, musicians and actors. Born in the northeastern part of the state, he moved to Bradenton-Sarasota, Florida for nearly 15 years where he wrote for a daily newspaper before moving his family back home to raise children on the prairies of South Dakota. He has visited the Black Hills dozens of times as a child, a parent, and now with his wife, Jane, as empty nesters.

Astoria

Astoria, Oregon was the West Coast's first permanent American settlement. The city and surrounding areas have been the location of choice for many Hollywood blockbusters as well as for vacationers looking to see the state's beautiful North Coast.

Price: $14.95; ISBN: 978-1-935455-08-0

Biloxi

Explore Biloxi and the Mississippi Gulf Coast. Find the best place to get a bowl of seafood gumbo and the most enjoyable golf course. From casinos to beaches, Biloxi and Gulfport offer great vacation opportunities.

Price: $14.95; ISBN: 978-1-935455-09-7

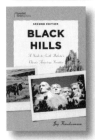

Black Hills (2nd Edition)

Revised and updated, use this guide to discover the striking natural beauty, abundant wildlife, and many attractions that the Black Hills has to offer, from the iconic Mount Rushmore to the historic Mammoth Site.

Price: $14.95; ISBN: 978-1-935455-10-3

Branson

Explore Branson, Missouri and the Ozarks. This completely independent guide will help you plan the perfect vacation, with information about the best shows in town and other attractions in the Lakes Area. Learn why many call Branson "America's favorite hometown."

Price: $14.95; ISBN: 978-1-935455-11-0

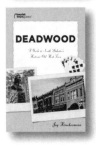

Deadwood

This independent book will help you plan the perfect vacation to the historic town of Deadwood, in the heart of South Dakota's Black Hills. Stroll the streets where Wild Bill Hickok and Calamity Jane once lived.

Price: $13.95; ISBN: 978-1-935455-22-6

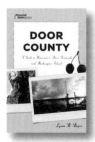

Door County

This independent guide will help you plan the perfect vacation to Wisconsin's thumb, including must-see attractions and the best outdoor activities. Hit the streets shopping, sit down for dinner overlooking the water, and discover the hidden natural beauty of Door County.

Price: $14.95; ISBN: 978-1-935455-12-7

Fredericksburg

Explore Fredericksburg's must-see attractions, find the best places for wine enthusiasts, and learn about the area's German heritage with this independent guide. Get the most out of your next visit to the Texas Hill Country.

Price: $14.95; ISBN: 978-1-935455-13-4

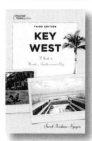

Key West (3rd Edition)

There is much to see and do in Key West, a vacation hotspot welcoming millions of visitors each year. In this guide, learn about area beaches, restaurants and bars, Duval Street attractions, hotels, and more. This book will help you plan your next vacation to the Conch Republic.

Price: $14.95; ISBN: 978-1-935455-14-1

Lake Placid

Look down a ski jump, hike the high peaks, and learn to dogsled. Explore the picturesque Village of Lake Placid, New York, and the surrounding Adirondacks. Also discover the best of nearby Lake George and Saranac Lake.

Price: $14.95; ISBN: 978-1-935455-15-8

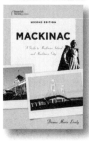

Mackinac (2nd Edition)

Nestled between Michigan's Upper and Lower Peninsulas, Mackinac Island is a favorite tourist destination and a beautiful getaway spot. This guide will help you plan your vacation to Mackinac Island and Mackinaw City.

Price: $14.95; ISBN: 978-1-935455-16-5

Madison County

Explore the picturesque landscape and historic covered bridges of Madison County, Iowa. Whether planning to photograph the bridges, sample the local wine, or take take a step back in time, make your journey a memorable one.

Price: $13.95; ISBN: 978-1-935455-17-2

Mystic

This guide to the historic Connecticut seaport city of Mystic will help you plan the perfect vacation, with comprehensive information about the Mystic Seaport, the best places to shop, dine and sleep, and must-see attractions.

Price: $14.95; ISBN: 978-1-935455-18-9

Salem

This independent guidebook will help you plan the perfect vacation to Massachusetts' historic seaport and site of the Salem Witch Trials, with information about the best historic attractions, Halloween and Haunted Happenings, and more.

Price: $14.95; ISBN: 978-1-935455-19-6

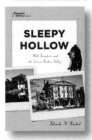

Sleepy Hollow

Washington Irving immortalized Sleepy Hollow and Tarrytown in his classic tale. This independent guide will help you plan the perfect vacation, with comprehensive information about must-see Historic Hudson Valley estates, facts and fictions of Sleepy Hollow, and more.

Price: $13.95; ISBN: 978-1-935455-20-2

Solvang

Plan the perfect vacation to America's Danish Capital. Learn about must-see area landmarks and highlights of the Santa Ynez Valley. From aebleskiver to vineyards and windmills, use this guide to travel prepared.

Price: $13.95; ISBN: 978-1-935455-21-9

Also Available

TITLE	ISBN	PRICE
Atlantic City	978-1-935455-00-2	$14.95
Breckenridge	978-0-9767064-9-6	$14.95
Frankenmuth	978-0-9767064-8-9	$13.95
Gatlinburg	978-1-935455-04-2	$14.95
Hershey	978-0-9792043-8-8	$13.95
Hilton Head	978-1-935455-06-6	$14.95
Jackson Hole	978-0-9792043-3-3	$14.95
Las Vegas	978-0-9792043-5-7	$14.95
Myrtle Beach	978-1-935455-01-1	$14.95
Niagara Falls	978-1-935455-03-5	$14.95
Ocean City	978-0-9767064-6-5	$13.95
Provincetown	978-1-935455-07-3	$13.95
Sandusky	978-0-9767064-5-8	$13.95
Williamsburg	978-1-935455-05-9	$14.95
Wisconsin Dells	978-0-9792043-9-5	$13.95

See http://www.touristtown.com for more information about any of these titles.

ORDER FORM

Telephone: With your credit card handy,
call toll-free 800.592.1566

Fax: Send this form toll-free to 866.794.5507

E-mail: Send the information on this form
to orders@channellake.com

Postal mail: Send this form with payment to Channel Lake, Inc.
P.O. Box 1771, New York, NY, 10156

Your Information: ( ) Do not add me to your mailing list

Name: _____

Address: _____

City: _____ State: _____ Zip: _____

Telephone: _____

E-mail: _____

Book Title(s) / ISBN(s) / Quantity / Price
(see www.touristtown.com for this information)

_____

_____

_____

Total payment*: $_____

Payment Information: (Circle One) Visa / Mastercard

Number: _____ Exp: _____

Or, make check payable to: **Channel Lake, Inc.**

* Add the lesser of $6.50 USD or 18% of the total purchase price for shipping. International orders call or e-mail first! New York orders add 8% sales tax.